# 100
## Literacy
## Hours

## YEAR 2

Published by Scholastic Ltd,
Villiers House,
Clarendon Avenue,
Leamington Spa,
Warwickshire CV32 5PR

© 1999 Scholastic Ltd

Text © 1999 David Waugh, Wendy Jolliffe
and Kathleen Taylor
3 4 5 6 7 8 9    0 1 2 3 4 5 6 7

SERIES CONCEPT
Chris Webster

AUTHORS
David Waugh
Wendy Jolliffe
Kathleen Taylor

EDITOR
Steven Carruthers

ASSISTANT EDITOR
Lesley Sudlow

SERIES DESIGNER
Joy White

DESIGNER
Rachel Warner

COVER ARTWORK
Peter Stevenson

ILLUSTRATIONS
Beverly Curl

British Library Cataloguing-in-Publication Data
A catalogue record for this book is available from the British Library.

ISBN 0-590-53978-7

The rights of David Waugh, Wendy Jolliffe and Kathleen Taylor to be
identified as the Authors of this work have been asserted by them in
accordance with the Copyright, Designs and Patents Act 1988.

ACKNOWLEDGEMENTS

The publishers gratefully acknowledge permission to reproduce the following copyright material:
**Bantam Doubleday Dell Publishing** for the use of 'What is Red?' by Mary O'Neill from *Hailstones and Halibut
Bones* © 1961, Mary Le Duc O'Neill (1961, Worlds's Work Limited and Doubleday and Company Inc).
**Egmont Children's Books Ltd** for the use of 'Sneezles' and 'Waiting at the Window' by AA Milne from *Now
We Are Six* by AA Milne © 1927, AA Milne (1927, Methuen).
**Faber & Faber** for the use of 'Monday's Child' by Catherine Storr from *Clever Polly and the Stupid Wolf* by
Catherine Storr (1955, Faber & Faber).
**Clive Riche** for the use of the poems 'A dog called Dog' and 'Eight? Great!' © 1999, Clive Riche,
previously unpublished.
**Anne Serraillier** for the use of 'The Rescue' by Ian Serraillier from *I'll Tell You A Tale* © 1976, Ian
Serraillier (1976, Puffin).

# Contents

# INTRODUCTION

## ABOUT THE SERIES

*100 Literacy Hours* is a series of year-specific teachers' resource books that provides a core of material for the teaching of the English curriculum within the context of the National Literacy Strategy *Framework for Teaching* and within the structure of the Literacy Hour. Each book offers term-by-term lesson plans, complete with objectives and organization grids and accompanied, where relevant, by photocopiable texts and activity sheets. The materials are ready-to-use, and their adaptable format enables them to be used as flexibly as possible. The 100 hours provided offer a balance of both reading and writing, and of range: fiction and poetry and non-fiction. However, it is expected that you will wish to personalize the material – altering the order, interleaving lesson plans with complementary materials from your school's existing schemes, consolidating work by using the structure of a lesson plan as a model for a lesson with different content, and so on. The loose-leaf format of each book, with hole-punched, perforated, tear-out pages, makes the integration of other tried-and-tested and favourite material into the core very easy.

## USING THE MATERIALS

### The materials

This book provides 100 literacy hours for Year 2, presented as 'units' of between 1 and 5 hours. There is a balance of reading and writing units, most of which are linked in order to demonstrate and reinforce the close relationship. The units are fully supported with detailed lesson plans and integrated photocopiable resources. Together, these materials should be regarded as a core, and a starting point for developing your own personalized folder for the year.

### Adapting and personalizing the materials

During the trialling of these resources, wide differences in ability were found in classes of the same year group in different schools. This means that the precise content of the plans and resources will almost certainly need modification to suit the pupils in a particular school. One way to do this is as follows:
■ Separate the pages of the book and place them in an A4 ringbinder.
■ Adjust the level of the photocopiable resource sheets to match the needs of the pupils in your year group.
■ 'Trade' materials with higher or lower year groups so that the average level matches that of the target year group.
■ Add your own favourite teaching materials in the appropriate places.
■ Substitute materials for others if necessary (for example, if you have a set of books which you wish to use instead of one of the ones recommended).
You will then have created a tailor-made folder of plans and resources for your year group.

### Preparing a scheme of work

All schools are required to write detailed schemes of work, and these materials have been designed to facilitate this process. The termly Overview Grids provided on pages 14–19 have been compiled by extracting the 'Objectives' grids from each teaching unit to provide you with what are, essentially, medium-term plans. These grids are photocopiable so, should you wish to alter the order of units and/or add your own, they can be copied, cut and pasted to make your own plans. On page 20 there is also a photocopiable set of blank objectives grids for you to use when inserting your own material.

## ORGANIZATION OF TEACHING UNITS

Each term is divided into teaching units comprising between 1–5 hours. Each of the main units has either a reading or a writing focus (although there is, of course, overlap) and a fiction, poetry or non-fiction content. The units are organized as follows:

## OBJECTIVES GRID

Outlines the word, sentence and text-level objectives of the unit.

| UNIT | SPELLING AND VOCABULARY | GRAMMAR AND PUNCTUATION | COMPREHENSION AND COMPOSITION |
|---|---|---|---|
| READING AND WRITING NON-FICTION Instructions and map directions. | Spell and use words appropriate for giving directions. | Write complete sentences using appropriate phrasing. | 'Read' a map. Write simple directions. |

## ORGANIZATION GRID

Outlines the key activities for each part of each hour.

| INTRODUCTION | WHOLE-CLASS SKILLS WORK | DIFFERENTIATED GROUP ACTIVITIES | CONCLUSION |
|---|---|---|---|
| **HOUR 1** Look at a steret map and give oral directions. | Learn to spell words associated with directions. Relate these to high frequency sight words – eg, *right* and *night*. | 1: Write directions using a street map. 2*: Read and sequence text. 3: Complete sentences which give directions. | Select pupils from each of the groups to read and present their work and discuss responses. Display a map with some directions. |
| **HOUR 2** Look at a street map and follow teacher's instructions. | Learn to spell words related to instuctions. | 1: Complete sentences which give directions. 2: Write directions using a street map. 3*: Read and sequence text. | Look at written directions and at key words and create a word bank. |

## UNIT LESSON PLANS

Each unit of lesson plans is written to the following headings:

### Resources
Provides a list of what you need for teaching the whole unit. Where appropriate, in the longer units, these have been grouped into paragraphs for ease of reference – eg common classroom resources, photocopiable pages, other items.

### Preparation
Outlines any advance preparation needed before the hour(s) begins – eg, any photocopying and/or enlarging of texts.

Each hour is then set out as follows:

### Introduction and whole-class skills work
Note: In the Overview Grids, the 'Introduction' and 'Whole-class skills work' sections are separate, whereas in the main text of the units, they are combined in one paragraph.
Introduction: Describes the activities for the whole-class shared reading/writing session.
Whole-class skills work: Describes the activities for the whole-class word- and sentence-level skills session. (See page 7 for further information about whole-class skills work.)

### Differentiated group activities
Describes the group activities for the guided group and independent work session. (See page 9 for further information about differentiated group work.)

### Conclusion
Sets out what to do in the whole-class plenary session.

### Photocopiables
Photocopiable texts and activity sheets are provided to support each unit. These can be found at the end of each relevant unit and are marked with the photocopiable symbol. Many of the sheets have more than one application and are therefore referred to in several units.

## READING UNITS

These teaching units have three aims:
- to develop basic reading skills across a wide range of texts - fiction, poetry and non-fiction
- to develop skills of comprehension at a literal and inferential level
- to encourage enjoyment of reading.

### Using the texts

Some texts are provided on photocopiable resource sheets. In addition, the following texts are either needed or are recommended:

- A copy of *The Highway Code*
- 'Mirror Poem' from *this poem doesn't rhyme* by Martyn Wiley and Ian McMillan ed. G. Benson, Puffin 1990
- A copy of the rhyme 'There Was an Old Woman Who Swallowed a Fly'
- 'Bedtime' by Eleanor Farjeon from *The Oxford Treasury of Children's Poems,* OUP 1989
- *Revolting Rhymes* by Roald Dahl, Picture Puffin 1984
- Large well-illustrated recipe books, including those for children.
- Simple rhyming dictionary
- Simple dictionary of synonyms and/or a simple dictionary of antonyms
- Baa Baa Black Sheep
- Any well-known traditional tale
- Versions of Little Red Riding Hood
- Selection of information and picture books at appropriate level, and Big Books
- Selection of newspapers and colour magazines
- Selection of alphabetically ordered books, especially catalogues, telephone directories, book with indexes, dictionaries
- Selection of chidren's encyclopμdias
- Simple reference books, eg New Way series
- Fiction in the present tense, eg Fuzzbuzz series
- Any piece of text containing a list of instructions (such as the instructions for self-assembly furniture)
- Any simple street map (possibly of an area known to the children)

Full details of these texts appear in the 'Resources' section of each unit. All of the texts are intended for use as shared texts; that is to say, texts for whole-class and/or guided reading. Use of appropriate teaching methods enables children to read and understand texts beyond their independent reading level. The methods suggested in these materials include:

- preparation: for example, giving the background to a story, prior study of difficult words
- shared reading to the whole class with children following the text
- differentiated follow-up activities which allow the most able children to respond independently to the text while further support is given to weaker readers
- guided reading, in which the teacher takes groups of pupils through the text helping them with phonic or contextual clues (less able readers), or higher-level reading skills (more able readers).

Additional suggestions are given, where relevant, in the detailed lesson plans – for example, use of different versions of the same story. It is assumed that children will be following a programme of guided reading alongside their reading of these shared texts.

### Written comprehension

Most written tasks included in these materials encourage a creative response to reading. These often reveal children's comprehension of the text as clearly as any formal comprehension, and, like the oral and dramatic activities, they are just as effective in developing comprehension skills. Activities included in the units will support the development of these skills.

## WRITING UNITS

The writing units provide a series of structured writing experiences throughout the year. Some writing will be done with the teachers or another adult, and some will be done with the teacher modelling writing, but using the children's suggestions. These shared writing sessions should enable the teacher to use the vocabulary of writing and to discuss approaches to presentation. The teacher should also be able to demonstrate that writing can be revised and redrafted to make it more accessible to an audience.

There are also many opportunities for children to write independently, but at Key Stage 1 it is particularly important to provide props such as word banks (see Additional Resources, page 9) and frameworks which children can draw upon. These props should enable the children to become more independent to allow the teacher more time to work with children during differentiated group sessions.

### Cross-curricular writing

Many opportunities for non-narrative writing occur in other curriculum areas. Therefore, when the necessary skills have been introduced through one of the non-fiction units, they should be applied to another curriculum area soon afterwards. There will be opportunities for this in history, religious education and science in particular.

### SPEAKING AND LISTENING

Speaking and Listening is also an essential part of literacy, and development of skills in this important area has been integrated into the units for both reading and writing. Speaking and Listening is the most important way of developing reading skills. Children need to explore texts through discussion, role play and other forms of oral 'comprehension' before they can write with greater understanding. 'Brainstorming', sharing ideas, helping each other to check work and so on, will all help pupils to write more effectively.

## TIMING OF THE LITERACY HOUR

A brisk pace is an important feature of an effective literacy hour. The following suggestions will help to keep things moving:

■ Train pupils to work independently. Tell them that you cannot help them while you are working with a group – their turn will come. In the meantime, they must find out for themselves, or ask a friend or a classroom assistant.

■ Keep explanations brief. Get pupils on task as soon as possible, and give further clarification and help in the context of the activity. The use of a Task Management Board may help by acting as a visual reminder of group tasks. This uses symbols to denote activities (which can be created by the class) and 'T' to denote when working with the teacher. Groups are listed or named down the left-hand side of the board and the symbols put alongside each group. If the symbols are laminated and backed with Velcro or Blu-Tack, they can be easily moved around and re-used. (For further details see NLS Training materials Module 1 'Practical Suggestions for Organised Directed Independent work'.)

■ Don't let skills sessions over-run, unless there is a good reason which has been planned for previously. Skills will be revised and practised several times throughout the year within the context of other slots in the Literacy Hour and in other lessons in English and other curricular areas.

■ When starting group activities sessions, give a clear message about what you want pupils to have achieved in the time allocated, and encourage them to work efficiently – ask them to concentrate on written task and complete illustrations later.

■ When working with a group, sit in a position so that the rest of the class can be seen.

■ Break off group work immediately to deal with any disruption. Ensure that children are aware that they are being supervised even when you are working with a group.

### Introductory session: Shared reading and Whole-class skills work

The following procedure is recommended:

■ Select a specific focus in advance (eg rhyming words).

■ Begin by predicting the contents of the text from the cover and title (and blurb if appropriate).

■ Discuss words in the title, look at the title page and other illustrations. (This is an important step in activating children's prior knowledge, which is vital in a meaningful learning context.)

■ Read the text at a brisk expressive pace with the children joining in and use a pointer to point to the words as you read. This will help to emphasize the one-to-one correspondence of one spoken word to one written word, and focus the children to the text. Ensure that you use a pointer, as fingers will mask the text.

■ During reading, stop occasionally (but not so frequently that the meaning is lost) to ask questions or predict what will happen next.

■ Demonstrate using different cues, for example, picture cues or graphophonic cues, ie 'How can we work out this tricky word?' You can also demonstrate reading on and leaving a word out, but guessing it later, or reading back to find out a difficult word, depending on the position of the word in the sentence.

■ After reading, respond to the text by asking questions to ensure understanding of the contents. Extend by asking questions which require an inferential understanding.

■ Focus upon specific sentence- or word-level aspects after ensuring an understanding of the whole text.

■ Use a variety of guided and independent tasks to deepen understanding, and to explore word- and sentence-level aspects. The units contain a large number of tasks of this nature.

It is during these sessions that grammar, punctuation, spelling, vocabulary and phonic skills are taught, with an emphasis upon word-level work at Key Stage One. The main principle is that the skills arise from the shared text and will also be used in the related writing Unit. Over the year, key skills should be revisited many times so that pupils' mastery of them will grow incrementally.

Although the materials in this book include spelling activities based upon spelling rules and patterns arising from the texts, they cannot take the place of a programme of individualized spelling for pupils. Pupils could collect, in a spelling book, a list of words they need to learn. This could be supplemented at least once a week with words from a standard list to make a list of, say, ten (or more for abler/older pupils). Pupils then learn their lists using the 'Look, say, cover, write, check' strategy. Pairs of pupils can test each other on their own lists. Any words not learned can be carried over into the next list.

At Key Stage One there should be considerable emphasis upon the following:

■ listening to the sounds within words and identifying phonemes;
■ identifying initial sounds;
■ simple mnemonics to help children to remember spellings;
■ spelling patterns;
■ segmenting words into onset and rime and into graphemes which represent phonemes.

## A NOTE ON TEACHING PHONICS

There are three main strands in the teaching of phonics:

### Phonological awareness

Children must be able to hear and discriminate sounds in words accurately. It is important to assess children's ability to do this and provide plenty of opportunities to develop the use of rhythm, rhyme and alliteration for those who have not yet developed good phonological awareness.

### Sound/symbol (Phoneme/grapheme) correspondence

One teaching programme which helps develop this correspondence is **THRASS** (Teaching Handwriting Reading and Spelling Skills). Central to THRASS is the chart which shows how all 44 sounds (phonemes) of spoken English are represented by letters (graphemes). THRASS focuses upon knowledge of the alphabet and the naming of the lower-case letters and their capitals, using the correct terms from the beginning (eg, phoneme and grapheme). THRASS also teaches that it is not always one letter which makes one sound (a graph); it may be two letters (a digraph) or three letters (a trigraph).

**Mnemonics:** Many phonic schemes (for example, *Letterland*, or *The Phonic Handbook: Jolly Phonics*) utilize mnemonics to help children to remember the sound/symbol relationship. These are useful as an interim measure in helping children to recall the letter and the sound(s) it makes.

**Blending/segmenting sounds:** Children need to be taught to blend individual phonemes into words when reading and to segment words into sounds for spelling in order to use phonics successfully.

## Differentiated group activities

For most group activities, three levels of differentiation are suggested:

Group 1:  above average pupils
Group 2:  average pupils
Group 3:  below average pupils

The ability groups may be further sub-divided according to the size of class and ability of the children. Groups do not have to be of equal size and there may be some flexibility of groupings.

In the average Key Stage One class, group sizes would be between 8-10 (with some trade-off between groups according to the spread of ability in the class). This is fine for organizational purposes, and working with the teacher, but too large for most collaborative activities. These groups will therefore need to be sub-divided into smaller groups of fours or pairs for some activities.

Try to divide your teaching time equally between all groups over the course of the week – the most able need help just as much as the least able if they are given suitably demanding tasks.

**[NB: An asterisk (*) after the group number is used on the grids and in the lesson plans to show which groups the teacher should be working with during the group activities session.]**

Finally, it is important to stress that even when you are working intensively with one group, the first priority is always the overall work rate of the whole class. See 'Timing of the Literacy Hour' (page 7) for suggestions on how to keep the session moving at a brisk pace.

## Finishing off

At the end of the group activities, it may be that some children have not completed their work. If this is the case, children should complete short tasks as homework. Some tasks may be completed over several sessions, for example if they are making their own books. However, it is important to stress to children what they are expected to finish within the time and thereby ensure the pace of work.

## Conclusion (plenary sessions)

The key objective in most of these sessions is to review the teaching points of the lesson and ensure that the work of selected pupils, pairs or groups is shared with the class for discussion and evaluation. Enough should be heard to exemplify the variety of work produced, but not so much that it becomes boring, or takes too much time. Keep a record of who has presented what to ensure that all pupils have the opportunity to present their work in due course.

# ASSESSMENT

Regular and on-going assessment of pupils' achievements and progress is, of course, essential. These materials assume that you and your school have satisfactory methods and systems of assessing and recording already in place and therefore don't attempt to suggest an alternative. However, what these materials also assume is that your current procedures are based on clearly stated teaching objectives. Therefore the objectives grids at the beginning of each unit should be invaluable in providing you with a framework for on-going assessment.

In addition, to facilitate individual pupil conferencing at the end of each half-term, a photocopiable record sheet has been provided on page 13. Specific targets for reading and writing can be set for each pupil at the end of the previous half-term and recorded on the sheet in the left-hand column. Interim progress towards these targets can be assessed when appropriate and noted in the middle column. Then, at the end of each half-term, during the conference, pupil and teacher together can record achievement and agree further targets for the next half-term.

# ADDITIONAL RESOURCES

The following additional equipment and resources are invaluable in delivering the Literacy Hour, and are referred to in a number of units:

- Big Book stand
- Whiteboard/magnetic board and letters
- Pointer (a home-made one will do!)
- OHP and acetate sheets
- Post-it notes
- Masking cards – which slide to reveal particular words (see below for details)
- Selection of ready made blank cards for writing key vocabulary
- Listening centre and headphones
- Blank Big Books
- Bank of frequently used resources for independent group work, eg word wheels, word dice, rhyming pictures, letter dice, words squares, sight word recognition games, eg lotto, pairs. A range of these resources is provided in these materials for specific activities.
- Resource box for each table, containing, eg spelling resources (spelling cards, dictionaries, personal dictionaries, 'have a go' books), pencils, crayons, sharpeners, rubbers, scissors, glue, highlighters.

### Enlarged Texts

A large variety of enlarged texts can be used for shared reading. For example commercially produced posters, nursery rhyme cards, and poems are available from publishers. Home-made posters and shaped poem cards can also be made by typing the text (again in 48-point font size) and adding illustrations from photocopiable sheets or children's own illustrations. Shaped poem cards are made by using an enlarged shape, such as that of a pig, and then fixing on a suitable poem or rhyme. Laminate or cover in sticky-back plastic for extended use. With the text extracts provided you can make enlarged versions simply by using the photocopier facility to enlarge to A3.

### Storyboards

An enlarged storyboard on which you can fix characters and objects from a story is very useful in order to focus young children on the story and help fix the details in their minds. To make one, use a large sheet of chipboard or hardboard measuring about 75cm high by 90cm wide and cover in felt. Now cut appropriate characters to fit the story out of different coloured felt, or use cardboard and attach a patch of Velcro to the back (you can build up a selection of characters for traditional tales). The characters will stick to the felt board. Alternatively, if you have a magnetic board, cut the characters or objects out of stiff cardboard and colour or paint and fix magnetic tape to the back of them. You can use enlarged photocopiable sheets for the characters, which can be coloured and cut out (see examples in photocopiables contained in this series).

### Word banks

Word banks can take many forms. You can provide lists of words which children will need for general use (for example, the high frequency lists in the National Literacy Strategy *Framework for Teaching* – reproduced as photocopiable page 182) and/or lists of words for specific activities or topics.

### How to make a word bank:

The words may be provided on sheets of paper or they may be displayed so that children can refer to them constantly and use them as part of their 'Look, say, cover, write, check' strategy.

You could make a pocket wall display. This will consist of a large piece of cloth (such as very strong cotton) approximately 1.5cm wide and 1m long, onto which are stitched pockets large enough to house high frequency words printed onto card. The letters of the alphabet in lower and

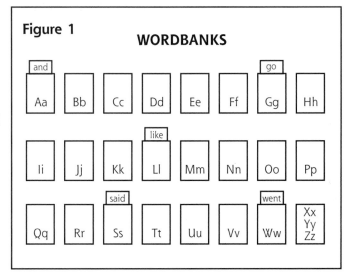

Figure 1

**WORDBANKS**

| and | | | | | | go | |
|-----|----|----|----|----|----|----|----|
| Aa | Bb | Cc | Dd | Ee | Ff | Gg | Hh |

| | | | like | | | | |
|----|----|----|----|----|----|----|----|
| Ii | Jj | Kk | Ll | Mm | Nn | Oo | Pp |

| | | said | | | | went | |
|----|----|----|----|----|----|----|-----|
| Qq | Rr | Ss | Tt | Uu | Vv | Ww | Xx Yy Zz |

upper case will need to be displayed on the outside of the pockets. (You could combine x y z on one pocket.) Alternatively this could be made from strong card with cardboard pockets (see Figure 1).

When new words are added, use the opportunity to discuss spelling and alphabetical order and ask the children to help you place the new words in the correct positions, Encourage the children to go to the word bank to see if spellings they need are displayed rather than asking you for your help. Discuss the words regularly and make sure the children become increasingly familiar with them.

## GENERAL BOOK MAKING

A range of book-making activities is used in the units. Instructions for these are follows:

### Zigzag book

Cut a strip of thick paper or thin card. This can be half a sheet of A3 cut lengthwise or bigger or smaller as required. Make even folds in the paper to create a concertina effect (Figure 2). Extra zigzag strips can be joined on with adhesive tape if more pages are required.

**Figure 2**

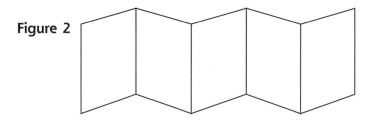

### Stapled book

Also known as 'little books', these are invaluable for story sequencing or story writing activities and can be made in different sizes and shapes. Start by working out how many pages are needed – remember that one folded sheet of paper will provide four pages. Take the appropriate number of sheets and fold each one exactly in half. Staple along the centre fold (Figure 3). To make a firmer cover, replace the outside sheet of paper with a piece of card. A laminated cover will help the book to last longer.

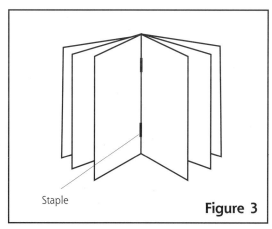

Staple

**Figure 3**

### Lift-the-flap book

Fold a sheet of A3 paper in half lengthways. Fold this in half again widthways and in half again (Figure 4). Cut flaps carefully with a craft knife or sharp scissors on alternate pages, making a total of three flaps.

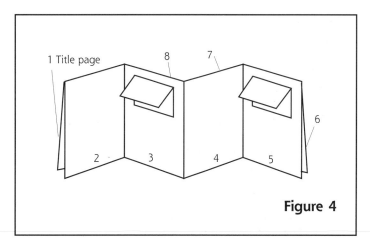

1 Title page

8

7

6

2    3    4    5

**Figure 4**

### Shape book

Make a card template of the shape you wish to use (keep the shape as simple as possible). Fold a sheet of card for the cover and enough cartridge paper to make the inside pages for one book, then use the template as an outline to cut through the whole book in one go (Figure 5a) and staple together.

Alternatively, you can make books with shaped covers only. To do this, trace round the template and cut several covers at once from card. Staple or sew each cover over the inside pages (Figure 5b).

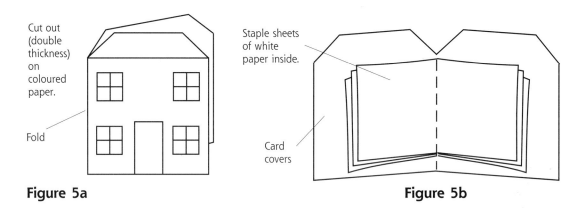

Cut out (double thickness) on coloured paper.

Fold

Staple sheets of white paper inside.

Card covers

**Figure 5a**                                                            **Figure 5b**

## USE OF AN OVERHEAD PROJECTOR

Having the use of an overhead projector (OHP) is ideal for whole-class work. Photocopiable texts and skills activities can then be copied onto acetate to make overhead transparencies (OHTs) which can be projected onto a screen or a bare, white or light-coloured wall, or a whiteboard which can then be written on. Where an OHP is not available, photocopiable sheets should be enlarged to at least A3 size with print at 48 point.

## INFORMATION AND COMPUTER TECHNOLOGY

The use of computers during the Literacy Hour is to be encouraged in a variety of ways:
■ For skills practice, using programs such as *Animated Alphabet*
■ For word processing, either by the teacher during shared or guided writing sessions, or by pupils using simpler word processing programmes, such as *Clicker Plus* (Crick Software) which enables the creation of grids similar to an overlay keyboard, but on screen
■ For creating own books and developing story writing using programs such as StoryBook Weaver (Iona Software)
■ For developing reading skills using interactive stories on CD-Rom.

### A NOTE ON PHOTOCOPYING

Please note that where there is instruction to copy material from copyright texts, you need to ensure that this is done within the limits of the copying licence your school has. If pupils are using their own exercise books or paper for answers, then all photocopiable resources are re-usable.

# PUPIL RECORD SHEET

| Pupil's name: | | | | Class | | Year group |
|---|---|---|---|---|---|---|
| Term | 1 | 2 | 3 | 1st half | | 2nd half |

| TARGET(S) | INTERIM PROGRESS (inc. dates) | ACHIEVEMENT AT END OF HALF TERM |
|---|---|---|
| Reading | | |
| Writing | | |

# OVERVIEW: YEAR 2
## TERM 1

| UNIT | SPELLING AND VOCABULARY | GRAMMAR AND PUNCTUATION | COMPREHENSION AND COMPOSITION |
|---|---|---|---|
| READING AND WRITING NON-FICTION Instructions and map directions. | Spell and use words appropriate for giving directions. Relate to high frequency sight words. | Write complete sentences using appropriate phrasing. | 'Read' a map. Write simple directions. |
| WRITING NON-FICTION Labelling diagrams. | Read and understand words related to a specific topic. | Understand that in labelling, the devices of prose such as full stops are not used. Use simple organizational devices such as keys. | Draw and label pictures and diagrams to show key parts of an object. |
| READING AND WRITING FICTION 'Lost in a Shop'. | Extend vocabulary from reading. | Revise knowledge of capital letters. Use awareness of grammar to decipher new or unfamiliar words. Discuss adjectives to describe characters. | Identify and discuss simple plot line. Understand time and sequential relationships in stories. |
| WRITING NON-FICTION 'Baking Bread'. | Collect and list time words. | Identify key words and phrases related to the language of time. | Use the language of time to structure a sequence of events. Write simple instructions. Use diagrams in instructions. |
| READING AND WRITING FICTION 'Charlie's A Good Boy Now!' | Make a word bank of words with the vowel phonemes from List 3 of the National Literacy Strategy – oo, ar, oy and ow. Learn to read and spell new words related to the story. | Predict words from preceding and surrounding words. | Use the context of reading as a cue to predict meanings of words and make sense of what they read. Understand time and sequential relationships in stories. Discuss reasons for events in stories linked to plot. Use story structure to write about own experiences in similar form. |

HOUR 2
HOUR 2
HOUR 5
HOUR 3
HOUR 5

# OVERVIEW: YEAR 2
## TERM 1 (CONTINUED)

| UNIT | SPELLING AND VOCABULARY | GRAMMAR AND PUNCTUATION | COMPREHENSION AND COMPOSITION |
|---|---|---|---|
| READING POETRY 'Monday's Child'. | Read high frequency words on sight. | Revise knowledge of capitalization. | Use story structure to write an alphabetical story. |
| READING AND WRITING POETRY 'Eight? Great!' and 'A dog called Dog'. | Investigate and classify words with the same sounds some of which have different spellings. Make a collection of these words. | Understand that capital letters are needed at the beginning of lines of poetry. Reorder sentences into a correct, logical sequence. | Read and write rhyming couplets. Write new lines for a poem. |
| READING FICTION AND POETRY 'An Alphabetical Story'. | Read high frequency words on sight. | Revise knowledge of capitalization. | Use story structure to write an alphabetical story. |
| READING AND WRITING NON-FICTION Directions and instructions. | Spell words frequently used in instructions. Collect and list new words from reading. | Find examples in non-fiction of words and phrases that link sentences. | Explain in writing how to play a game. Read simple directions. |
| READING FICTION 'Chloe and Jack'. | Understand and identify words which require capital letters. | Recognize and take account of capital letters and full stops to read aloud with appropriate expression. | Use grammatical cues to predict where punctuation should be placed. |
| READING AND WRITING NON-FICTION Recipes. | Collect and list new words from reading. | Understand how points can be listed and the sequential nature of directions. Focus upon the language of instruction. | Read simple directions for making things. Write simple directions for cooking using the appropriate register. |

HOUR 1
HOUR 3
HOUR 2
HOUR 5
HOUR 3
HOUR 2

# OVERVIEW: YEAR 2
## TERM 2

| UNIT | SPELLING AND VOCABULARY | GRAMMAR AND PUNCTUATION | COMPREHENSION AND COMPOSITION |
|---|---|---|---|
| READING FICTION 'Chloe Confused'. | Use phonic and word recognition. | Make use of punctuation to aid reading with expression. | Shared reading of a story. |
| READING AND WRITING FICTION 'Sneezles' and 'Waiting at the Window'. | Read and spell words containing the digraphs *wh* and *ph*. Learn new words from spelling. | Use awareness of grammar to decipher unfamiliar and invented words. Read aloud with intonation and expression. | Develop an understanding of the language of poetry. Use structures from poetry as a basis for writing. Recite a poem taking account of punctuation. |
| READING POETRY 'My Shadow'. | Make a collection of unfamiliar words. | Read own writing. Check for grammatical sense and accuracy. Predict from text. | Use structure from poems as a basis for writing. |
| READING AND WRITING FICTION AND POETRY 'Words Within Words'. | Split compound words into their component parts. | Use awareness of grammar to decipher unfamiliar words. Read aloud with intonation and expression appropriate to grammar and punctuation. | Use phonological, contextual and graphic knowledge when reading texts. Make a glossary of compound words. Write a story and discuss a poem. |
| READING FICTION AND POETRY 'Bedtime' and 'Four Apples Fall'. | Understand that some words have the same sounds but different spellings (homophones). Explore sets of words with different spellings of the same phoneme. | Use simple sentences to write a simple ending. | Read a poem and consider rhymes. Predict a story ending from an unfinished extract. |
| READING FICTION AND POETRY Alphabetical and other lists. | Discriminate syllables orally and in writing. | Investigate other ways of presenting texts. | Identify features of sound in poems. |
| READING AND WRITING FICTION 'Who am I?' | Segment words into phonemes for spelling. | Identify speech marks in reading. Understand their purpose and use terms correctly. | Prepare and re-tell stories through role play in groups using dialogue and narrative from text. |
| READING POETRY 'The Rescue'. | Create a word bank of rhyming words. Classify words with the same sounds but different spellings. | Identify key words and phrases. | Raise awareness of differences between story and poetic language. |

# OVERVIEW: YEAR 2
## TERM 2 (CONTINUED)

| UNIT | SPELLING AND VOCABULARY | GRAMMAR AND PUNCTUATION | COMPREHENSION AND COMPOSITION |
|------|--------------------------|--------------------------|-------------------------------|
| READING AND WRITING FICTION 'Little Red Riding Hood' and other traditional stories. | Learn new words linked to a story. Revise the use of the grapheme oo (short as in *good* and long as in *moon*). | Secure the use of simple sentences in own writing. Use commas to separate items in a list. Use speech marks in dialogue. | Identify and describe characters in a story. Write a story in the same setting as 'Little Red Riding Hood'. Discuss story settings and talk about their influence upon events and behaviour. |
| READING FICTION 'Getting Ready for School'. | Learn new words related to a particular topic. | Use a variety of ways of presenting texts. | Use flow charts to explain a process. |
| READING AND WRITING FICTION 'Swimming after school'. | Spell words with common prefixes to indicate the negative. Explore the use of antonyms. | Use awareness of grammar to decipher new words. Explore the need for grammatical agreement in writing. | Use phonological, contextual, grammatical and graphic knowledge to work out, predict and check the meanings of unfamiliar words. Use shared and guided writing to apply phonological and graphic knowledge and sight vocabulary to spell words accurately. Reinforce and apply word level skills through shared reading. |
| READING AND WRITING POETRY 'What is Red?' | Segment words into phonemes for spelling. | Re-read own writing to check that it makes sense. | Use simple poem structures to write poems collectively and individually. |
| READING AND WRITING FICTION 'A Funny Thing Happened'. | Read on sight words from the high frequency List 1. | Predict words from preceding words. | Use context as a cue when reading. Predict story endings. Identify and describe characters. Use a story setting and write a different story in the same setting. |

# OVERVIEW: YEAR 2
## TERM 3

| UNIT | SPELLING AND VOCABULARY | GRAMMAR AND PUNCTUATION | COMPREHENSION AND COMPOSITION |
|---|---|---|---|
| READING FICTION Tongue-twisters and alliteration. | Revise work on homophones. Learn new words linked to writing. | Read text aloud with intonation and expression. | Write alliterative sentences. |
| READING FICTION 'Jack and the Beanstalk'. | Learn new words linked to a story. | Turn statements into questions. Understand the use of question marks and other punctuation. | Retell a story using a flow chart. |
| READING FICTION 'Mrs Leach and the Leaks'. | Discriminate, read and spell the phonemes ea (long as in hear) and ea (short as in head). Identify other ways in which the digraph ea may be sounded in commonly used words. | Read text aloud with intonation and expression appropriate to the grammar and punctuation. | Reinforce and apply word level skills through shared and guided reading. |
| READING AND WRITING NON-FICTION 'Animals' and 'Fact or Fiction?' | Learn new words related to a topic. Discuss spelling and sounds. Use synonyms to aid understanding of new words. | Write in clear sentences using capital letters, full stops and question marks accurately. | Understand the distinction between fact and fiction. Pose questions and record them in writing. Scan a text and look for key words and phrases and sub-headings. |
| READING NON-FICTION Indexes. | Learn new words related to a topic. Secure reading and spelling of pupils' names. | Reinforce the use of commas in lists. | Examine a range of ordered texts. Discus how and why they are used. Use an index to move around text. |
| READING AND WRITING NON-FICTION Information from book covers. | Learn new words related to a topic. | Write in clear sentences using capital letters, full stops and questions marks accurately. | Read about authors from information on book covers. Raise awareness of authorship and publication. |

# OVERVIEW: YEAR 2
## TERM 3 (CONTINUED)

| UNIT | SPELLING AND VOCABULARY | GRAMMAR AND PUNCTUATION | COMPREHENSION AND COMPOSITION |
|---|---|---|---|
| WRITING NON-FICTION Questions. | Spell words beginning with the phoneme *wh*. Recognize and form questions using *what, why, where, which* and *who*. | Write in clear sentences using capital letters and full stops accurately. Turn statements into questions. Use question marks. | Reinforce and apply word level skills through shared and guided reading. Apply phonological, graphic knowledge and sight vocabulary to spell words accurately. |
| READING AND WRITING FICTION 'A Night Out'. | Secure knowledge of the spellings of the words in List 1 of the National Literacy Strategy. | Read aloud with intonation and expression. | Reinforce and apply word level skills through shared and guided reading. Apply phonological, graphic knowledge and sight vocabulary to spell words accurately. |
| READING AND WRITING NON-FICTION Word recognition and graphic knowledge. | Spell words with common suffixes. | Use standard forms of verbs in speaking and writing. | Reinforce and apply word level skills through shared and guided reading. |
| READING FICTION AND POETRY 'Clare and Tim'. | Secure reading and spelling of high frequency words. | Use the past tense consistently for narration. | Notice the difference between spoken and written forms. |
| READING FICTION AND POETRY Textual examination. | Reinforce work on discriminating syllables in reading and spelling. Secure phonemic spellings from the previous five terms. | Understand the use of capital letters and full stops. | Develop phonological, contextual and grammatical knowledge by demonstrating that letters can have different sounds according to context. |

# OBJECTIVES GRIDS
## BLANK TEMPLATES

Use these photocopiable grids when inserting your own material.

| UNIT | SPELLING AND VOCABULARY | GRAMMAR AND PUNCTUATION | COMPREHENSION AND COMPOSITION |
|------|--------------------------|--------------------------|--------------------------------|
|      |                          |                          |                                |

| UNIT | SPELLING AND VOCABULARY | GRAMMAR AND PUNCTUATION | COMPREHENSION AND COMPOSITION |
|------|--------------------------|--------------------------|--------------------------------|
|      |                          |                          |                                |

| UNIT | SPELLING AND VOCABULARY | GRAMMAR AND PUNCTUATION | COMPREHENSION AND COMPOSITION |
|------|--------------------------|--------------------------|--------------------------------|
|      |                          |                          |                                |

| UNIT | SPELLING AND VOCABULARY | GRAMMAR AND PUNCTUATION | COMPREHENSION AND COMPOSITION |
|------|--------------------------|--------------------------|--------------------------------|
|      |                          |                          |                                |

Term 1

# RIGHT THIS WAY

## OBJECTIVES

| UNIT | SPELLING AND VOCABULARY | GRAMMAR AND PUNCTUATION | COMPREHENSION AND COMPOSITION |
|---|---|---|---|
| READING AND WRITING NON-FICTION Instructions and map directions. | Spell and use words appropriate for giving directions. Relate to high frequency sight words. | Write complete sentences using appropriate phrasing. | 'Read' a map. Write simple directions. |

## ORGANIZATION (2 HOURS)

| | INTRODUCTION | WHOLE-CLASS SKILLS WORK | DIFFERENTIATED GROUP ACTIVITIES | CONCLUSION |
|---|---|---|---|---|
| HOUR 1 | Look at a street map and give oral directions. | Learn to spell words associated with directions. Relate these to high frequency sight words – eg, *right* and *night*. | 1: Write directions using a street map. 2*: Read and sequence text. 3: Complete sentences which give directions. | Select pupils from each of the groups to read and present their work and discuss responses. Display a map with some directions. |
| HOUR 2 | Look at a street map and follow teacher's written instructions. | Learn to spell words related to instructions. | 1: Complete sentences which give directions. 2: Write directions using a street map. 3*: Read and sequence text. | Look at written directions and at key words and create a word bank. |

## RESOURCES

Photocopiable page 24 (Street Map), large-scale street map (this may be an actual map of an area known to the children, or it could be a simple map which you draw on the board, or you may wish to use an enlarged version of the photocopiable map provided), a set of sentences which give directions, a set of sentences which give directions but which are incomplete, board or flip chart, pointer, writing materials.

## PREPARATION

Make enough photocopies of page 24 for one between two children. Label and display the large-scale street map, or draw a map on the board or enlarge the photocopiable page for this purpose. Prepare two sets of sentence cards with directions written on, one set with the directions incomplete.

### Introduction and whole-class skills work

Show the children a simple street map which has various places labelled. Choose two places and ask the children how they would get from one place to the other. Ask children to come out and use a pointer as they give directions. You will need to reinforce the ideas of left and right and explain that the map is vertical, whereas in real life the streets would be horizontal. Encourage them to use phrases such as 'Turn left', 'Take the second turning on the left', and 'Turn right at the junction'. Write some of the key words which they will need on the board. In particular, look at the spelling of the word 'right' and relate this to 'night' which appears in List 1 of the National Literacy Strategy. This would also be an opportunity to look at 'light', 'sight', 'tight', 'bright' and other common words in this family.

### Differentiated group activities

1: Using photocopiable page 24 (Street Map), ask the children to choose different points on the map and to describe the route from one to another using key directional phrases.

2*: Provide the children with sentence cards which describe the route from one place to another on the map used. This should include directions and details of the places which are passed on the route. The sentences should be presented in the wrong order and the children will need to reorder them correctly. They might do this by physically rearranging the sentences after cutting them out, or they could write the sentences out.

3: Provide this group with the set of cards with incomplete sentences which give directions from one place to another on the map used. You will be able to gauge the extent to which you can miss out words. You might concentrate upon left and right or you could omit other phrases such as 'turn', 'go past' and 'cross over'.

   If a map program is available, some pairs of children could use the computer for this activity.

### Conclusion

Bring the children together to look at the map and ask each group to tell the class something about the ways in which they used directions. Discuss again, some of the vocabulary which is used when giving directions. Display the map plus some of the directions produced by the children.

### Introduction and whole-class skills work

Begin by showing the children the photocopiable map and writing directions on the board. Ask the children to read the directions carefully and try to work out the route which is being given. For example, you might start with 'Stand outside the church and look right down the road to the school. Walk towards the school but take the first turning on your right before you get there'. This should continue with instructions being written one at a time and children being encouraged to read them with the teacher. Follow this up by asking children to make up directions and by writing these on the board one by one. Once again, look at some of the words which are used in giving directions and help the children to learn how to spell them. Words which may feature and which also appear in the high frequency word list include:

| | | | | | | |
|---|---|---|---|---|---|---|
| about | after | back | by | down | first | from |
| half | house | just | next | one | over | school |
| take | then | two | way | when | where | |

When teaching children to spell the words, look constantly for examples of other words from the same families so that children may learn to apply the knowledge of spelling which they gain to a wider vocabulary.

### Differentiated group activities

1: Sentence completion activity (as Group 3, Hour 1).
2: Activity using street map (as Group 1, Hour 1).
3*: Sequencing text activity (as Group 2, Hour 1).

### Conclusion

Use this time to discuss the directions which Groups 1 and 2 have produced during the two lessons. Talk about the importance of accuracy and precision. Spend time looking again at the spelling of words which are used in directions and create a class word bank (see 'How to make a word bank', page 10 of the Introduction).

# STREET MAP

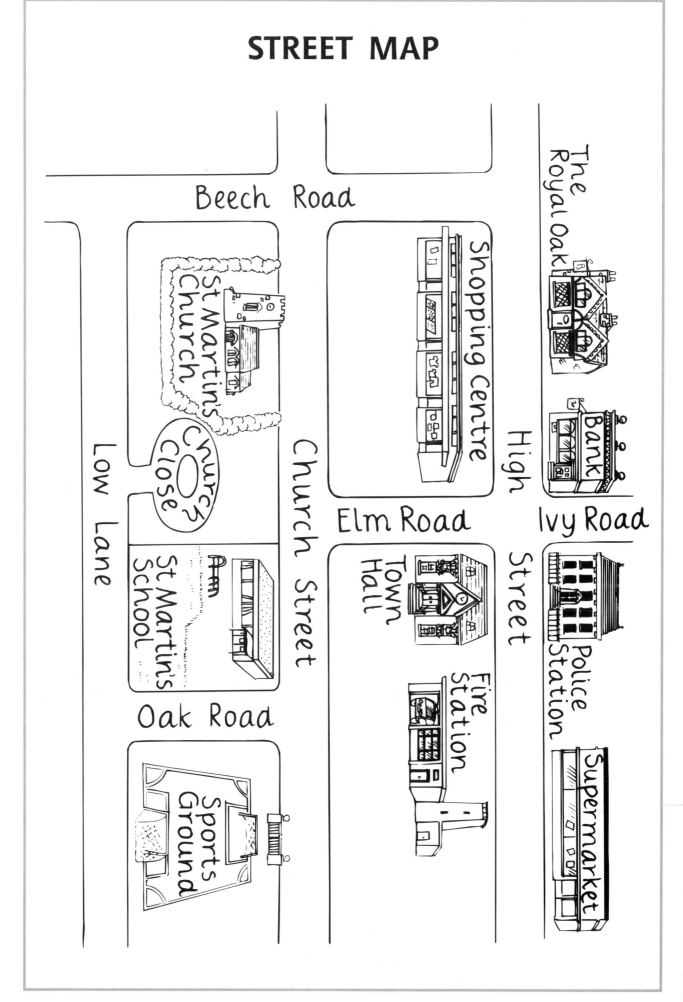

# LABEL IT!

## OBJECTIVES

| UNIT | SPELLING AND VOCABULARY | GRAMMAR AND PUNCTUATION | COMPREHENSION AND COMPOSITION |
|------|------|------|------|
| WRITING NON-FICTION Labelling diagrams. | Read and understand words related to a specific topic. | Understand that in labelling, the devices of prose such as full stops are not used. Use simple organizational devices such as keys. | Draw and label pictures and diagrams to show key parts of an object. |

## ORGANIZATION (2 HOURS)

| | INTRODUCTION | WHOLE-CLASS SKILLS WORK | DIFFERENTIATED GROUP ACTIVITIES | CONCLUSION |
|------|------|------|------|------|
| **HOUR 1** | Suggest labels for a picture. | Develop reading and raise phonological awareness by examining words on labels carefully. | 1: Label a picture of a house using partially completed words in a word bank. 2*: Draw and label a house with special features. 3: Label a picture of a house using a word bank. | Select pupils from each of the groups to read and present their work and discuss responses. Discuss the differences between labels and other writing. Display labelled pictures. |
| **HOUR 2** | Look at pictures labelled with keys. | Look at ways in which a key may be designed and used. | 1*: Look at pictures and diagrams with keys and discuss what they show. 2: Draw and label pictures using a key. 3: Label a simple, prepared picture with numbers or letters and writing a key. | All groups to show, display and explain their labelled pictures. |

## RESOURCES

A simple picture of a house, a simple picture or diagram of something else familiar to the children (such as a car or something related to work the children are doing in another subject area), Post-It notes or card and Blu-Tack, photocopiable pages 27 and 28 (A House), dictionaries, writing and drawing materials, board or flip chart, a selection of labelled and keyed pictures and diagrams from non-fiction books, newspapers and magazines (and, if possible, diagrams on the computer), card for preparing a word bank (see 'How to make a word bank', page 10 of the Introduction), a simple picture or diagram (for Group 3 in Hour 2).

## PREPARATION

Enlarge the simple pictures of a house and car (or similar) so that they can be used for whole-class work. Make enough copies of photocopiable pages 27 and 28 (A House) for two groups of children. Make a collection of labelled and keyed diagrams from different sources (for example, non-fiction books, newspapers and magazines, computer printouts).

### Introduction and whole-class skills work

Show the children the enlarged, simple picture of a house and ask them to tell you what the different parts of the house are called. As they do so, ask them which letters and sounds they think each of the parts begins with. Each time the children tell you the name of the part of the house, attach a label to the picture (using Post-It notes or card and Blu-Tack) or write the name next to the part, drawing attention to the spellings as you write. You may need to draw a line from the house to the label in order to ensure that there is sufficient room for all of the labels and that the picture does not become too cluttered.

Discuss the words which the children have provided and reinforce spelling of each word. Create a word bank of words including:

| | | | | |
|---|---|---|---|---|
| *house* | *door* | *home* | *window* | *roof* |
| *chimney* | *tree* | *garden* | *garage* | |

### Differentiated group activities

1: Provide the group with copies of photocopiable pages 27 and 28. Ask the children to label the house completing the words as they do so, with the help of a dictionary. Some pairs of children could use the computer spellchecker for this activity.

2\*: Ask each member of the group to draw a house of their own design and to label the parts. Tell them that they may include special features which they would like to have in their house, such as a swimming pool, a satellite dish or even a helipad.

3: Labelling activity using photocopiable pages 27 and 28, as Group 1 above. The children may also label parts for which words have not been provided, but they should try out spellings first and discuss these.

### Conclusion

Ask members of each group to show their labelled pictures to the rest of the class. Discuss with the children the way in which labels differ from ordinary writing (for example, by being printed or written in block capitals, and by not always being complete sentences). Display the children's labelled pictures.

### Introduction and whole-class skills work

Begin by discussing the labelled pictures which the children saw and made during the previous lesson. Discuss the way in which labelling can sometimes be restricted by lack of space, and ask if anyone has a suggestion to remedy the problem.

Introduce the children to a simple key by showing them a picture or diagram (for example, one of a car, or one related to the work the children are doing in another area) and labelling it with numbers or letters. Ask the children if they can tell what you are doing and invite them to tell you which words correspond to the letters or numbers. As they suggest these, write them on the board or flip chart and help children to spell the words.

Talk about ways in which a key may be presented and emphasize the importance of careful labelling and clear, neat writing.

### Differentiated group activities

1\*: Provide the children with a selection of pictures and diagrams from the library (from non-fiction books, newspapers and magazines and, if possible, diagrams on the computer). Discuss with the children the different types of keys and what they show.

2: Ask the children to draw and label a diagram of their own choice using a key. Encourage the children to present work carefully and, if necessary, provide them with a word bank to help them.

3: Provide the children with a simple picture or diagram and ask them to use numbers or letters to label it and then produce a key. You may need to provide them with a bank of appropriate words.

### Conclusion

Use this time to discuss the pictures and diagrams which the children have looked at or produced themselves during the two lessons. Present the work done to the class, discuss any problems with keys that may have been encountered, and review the key points covered. Display the labelled pictures.

# A HOUSE

# A HOUSE (CONTINUED)

■ Cut up these words and use them as labels for the picture of A House.

door

window

roof

chimney

garden

tree

path

gate

fence

wall

garage

drainpipe

# Lost In A Shop

## OBJECTIVES

| UNIT | SPELLING AND VOCABULARY | GRAMMAR AND PUNCTUATION | COMPREHENSION AND COMPOSITION |
|---|---|---|---|
| READING AND WRITING FICTION 'Lost in a Shop'. | Extend vocabulary from reading. | Revise knowledge of capital letters. Use awareness of grammar to decipher new or unfamiliar words. Discuss adjectives to describe characters. | Identify and discuss simple plot line. Understand time and sequential relationships in stories. |

## ORGANIZATION (5 HOURS)

| | INTRODUCTION | WHOLE-CLASS SKILLS WORK | DIFFERENTIATED GROUP ACTIVITIES | CONCLUSION |
|---|---|---|---|---|
| HOUR 1 | Shared reading of the story 'Lost in a Shop'. | Develop vocabulary and raise awareness of story structure. Discuss compound words. | 1: Read story and write sentences about each character. 2: Shared reading of text and selection of key points. 3*: Guided reading of text. Explore structure. Summarize key points. | Shared discussion about the key points of the story. Display key sentences. |
| HOUR 2 | Shared re-reading of the story 'Lost in a Shop'. | Focus upon new words learned in Hour 1. | 1*: Guided reading of text and selection of key points. 2: Re-read story and write sentences about each character. 3: Re-read the story and prepare to retell in their own words based upon notes. | Group 3 retelling the story in their own words. Class discussion. |
| HOUR 3 | Exploring the plot of 'Lost in a Shop' and discussing an ending for it. | Focus upon and learn to spell high frequency words from the text. | 1: Write an ending to the story. 2: Identify high frequency words in the text. 3*: Guided discussion about and writing an ending to the story. | Listening to and shared discussion about endings to the story. |
| HOUR 4 | Shared discussion of the key events of the story. | Build a collection of significant words in preparation for writing. | 1*: Write stories about being lost. 2: Write sentences about being lost. 3: Re-read the text and use a word bank to write sentences about each character. | Shared discussion about the characters and appropriate adjectives. |
| HOUR 5 | Shared discussion and writing about the story. | Investigate words with the same sounds but different spellings. | 1: Continuation of writing of stories. Check spelling and punctuation. 2*: Write short stories about being lost. 3: Write sentences about being lost. | Shared discussion of Group 2's story structures and suggestions for completing them. |

## RESOURCES

Photocopiable pages 33 and 34 ('Lost in a Shop'), a copy of List 1 of high frequency words from the National Literacy Strategy, list of characters in the story, board or flip chart, highlighter pens, other writing materials.

## PREPARATION

Make enough copies of photocopiable pages 33 and 34 ('Lost in a Shop') for each child to have a copy of the story. Prepare one enlarged copy on A3 paper. Prepare a sheet of the words in List 1 and make enough copies for Group 2. Prepare a list of the names of characters from the story (allowing sufficient space for the children to write about each one) and make enough copies for each child.

**Note:** The story includes many words which the children will already have met through their work on List 1. However, there are some words which may be less familiar and which they will need to understand if they are to manage the activities successfully. The word cards will help the children to learn these words.

### Introduction and whole-class skills work

Tell the children that you are going to read a story to them once and that you will then re-read it to them as they follow the text. Ask them to think carefully about the story as they listen and ask them to try to pick out the main events.

After reading the story once, show the children the story on screen or on the board. Before reading it with them, ask them if they can tell you who the main characters are. Do they know that the characters' names will have capital letters? Do they know that some of the words with capital letters are at the beginnings of sentences?

Read the story with the children and ask them to look out for the key events. Ask them to tell you of any words which they do not know or understand and write these on the board or show them to the children written on card. Talk about the sounds within the words and break the words up where possible to show how they fit together. Talk about compound words such as 'whatever', 'birthday', 'loudspeaker' and 'gentlemen', and show the children how it is sometimes possible to read longer words by looking for shorter words within them.

### Differentiated group activities

1: Give the children a sheet with the names of the main characters and ask them to write a sentence about each one, telling something about the character and his or her role in the story. Some pairs of children could use the computer for this activity.

2: Give the children a copy of the story and ask them, in pairs, to re-read it and pick out the most important sentences and underline or highlight them. When they have done this they should write the sentences out carefully in the correct order.

3*: Give the children a copy of the story and re-read it to them. Ask them to decide what the key events are. They should underline or highlight these and then write their own sentences to summarize the story.

### Conclusion

Each group should show an example of work and talk about what they have done. Encourage children to debate which were the key points in the story and make a list of these on the board based upon the children's ideas.

### Introduction and whole-class skills work

Begin by re-reading the story, 'Lost in a Shop', and ask the children to talk about the characters and their attributes. Group 1's work from the previous lesson may provide a starting point for discussion. Make a note on the board of adjectives which the children suggest are particularly appropriate for each character and discuss the spellings of the words as you do so.

Talk with the children about the phrases, clauses and sentences within the text which support their views of the characters. Look closely at any new words and discuss the ways in which the graphemes represent the phonemes. Many of the words in the story which may be unfamiliar to the children are phonically regular. You might focus upon some or all of the following:

| | | | | | |
|---|---|---|---|---|---|
| *allowed* | *collect* | *surprise* | *decided* | *peered* | *except* |
| *awful* | *shoulder* | *badge* | *voice* | *special* | *appeared* |
| *secret* | *forgiven* | *bought* | *department* | | |

Break the words up to show how the sounds fit together. You can do this by covering all but the part of the word on which you are concentrating. Encourage the children to think of other words which have similar sounds and show them that the phonemes may be represented in similar and sometimes different ways. For example, when talking about 'allowed' the children may easily confuse the word with 'aloud'. This would provide an opportunity to talk about different ways of making the 'ow' sound in 'cow'. Encourage further discussion of the vowel phonemes in List 3 of the National Literacy Strategy.

### Differentiated group activities

1*: Guided reading and discussion activity. Ask the children to tell you the story in their own words and make a note of the key events which they identify. Next, ask them to find these key points in the story.

2: Ask the children to re-read the text and to write sentences about each character. Encourage the children not only to make use of the work done on the board during the introductory session, but also to think of ideas of their own.

3: Ask the children to re-read the text and prepare to tell the story in their own words. Encourage them to make notes to help them to do this, but make it clear that they should not attempt to copy out whole chunks of text.

### Conclusion

Ask Group 3 to tell the story in their own words and discuss their interpretations with the rest of the class.

### Introduction and whole-class skills work

Begin by re-reading the story and talking to the children briefly about what has happened so far. Next, ask them what they think would happen on Tom's birthday. Ask the children to suggest what kind of present Tom might receive and encourage them to think about how he would react when his parents gave it to him. You might ask one or two children to come out to the front of the class and show how they would react.

Discuss with the children the qualities of a good ending to a story. Some may prefer stories which have a neat ending which sums everything up, while others may like endings which leave the reader with something to think about. You might go on to discuss endings of stories which they have read or heard, especially traditional tales such as Goldilocks.

Discuss again, some of the words which the children learned in the previous lesson, and draw their attention to some of the words from the high frequency List 1 which appear in the story (such as 'would', 'next', 'did' and 'saw').

### Differentiated group activities

1: Encourage the children to think about how they would like to end the story and ask them to write it down. They might jot down some ideas, particularly about Tom's present, before writing in sentences.

2: Provide this group with a copy of List 1 and ask the children to find as many of the words as they can in the text. As they find a word they should highlight it on their lists. When they find the word again they could begin a tally chart next to the words. This would help to emphasize the frequency with which some words occur and would help to stress the need for the children to learn the words.

3*: Discuss with the children an ending to the story. You may act as scribe for their ideas, in which case you should make a point of demonstrating how authors work by using a dictionary, making notes and revising and editing.

### Conclusion

Discuss the endings for the story which Groups 1 and 3 have produced. Highlight any words which have been used by Group 1 which the rest of the class could learn to spell together and focus upon any words which Group 3 used which you had to offer particular help with spelling.

### Introduction and whole-class skills work

Re-read the story but add some of the endings suggested by the children in the previous lesson. Talk with the children about the key events in the completed story.

Explain that some children will be writing about being lost and that you want to make sure that they have a bank of useful words available to them. Ask the children to suggest some words which they may wish to use. Where these also appear on List 1, draw the children's attention to this. Where words have not yet been discussed in this series of lessons, show the children how they are spelled and discuss their structures. If the children do not suggest many words, you might offer some such as:

| | | | |
|---|---|---|---|
| *frightened* | *terrified* | *scared* | *telephone* |
| *address* | *person* | *missing* | *vanished* |

### Differentiated group activities

1*: Tell the children that you want them to write stories about being lost. Ask them to think in particular about how they would feel and to try to describe this. They will be continuing this in Hour 5.

2: Ask the children to think carefully about what it might be like to be lost. They may have experienced this at some time. Ask them to write sentences about what it would be like to be lost.

3: Ask the children to re-read the story and write sentences about each character with the support of a word bank (see 'How to make a word bank', page 10 of the Introduction).

### Conclusion

Discuss with the whole class the experience of being lost, and write key words that the children suggest on the board. Draw attention to their spelling.

### Introduction and whole-class skills work

The final lesson of this unit involves groups undertaking tasks which others have previously attempted. You will need to spend time discussing some of the problems which were encountered and drawing attention to words which were misspelled.

Begin the lesson by talking about the stories the children wrote from their own experiences and compare them with 'Lost in a Shop'. Talk with the children about words which they think might be useful when they write and make a list of these so that they have a word bank on which to draw.

### Differentiated group activities

1: Ask the children to continue their stories about being lost. As they finish, encourage them to re-read their work and to check their use of capital letters and full stops and to use the text 'Lost in a Shop' to help them check spellings.

2*: Ask the children to expand the sentences they wrote during the previous lesson into short stories about being lost.

3: Ask the children to write sentences about being lost (as Group 2, Hour 4).

### Conclusion

Talk with the children about the stories which Group 2 wrote and encourage them to make suggestions for developing and improving the work. Draw attention again to terms such as character and plot and write on the board or flip chart some of the new words which have been learned during the week.

# LOST IN A SHOP

Tom Smith's mother and father were standing next to the till in the toy shop paying for something. Tom was not allowed to see what it was.

"Just look at the games and wait until we come and collect you," his father had said.

Tom couldn't help trying to see what it was his parents were buying, but he knew that it was something for his birthday, so he didn't really want to spoil the surprise.

When he had grown tired of looking at the games, he decided his mother and father must surely have finished paying for the toy by now and he peered round the corner of the shelves to see them.

They had gone! There was no one at the till except the lady who took the money. Tom looked around him. He looked down every row of shelves in the toy shop, but he could not see his parents anywhere. This was awful. He didn't know what to do. He stood in the middle of the shop and began to cry.

Suddenly, he felt a hand on his shoulder. "What's the matter, dear?" said a kindly voice. Tom looked around to see the lady who had been sitting at the till. He had always been told never to talk to strangers, so he didn't say anything to the lady.

"Have you lost your mummy and daddy?" asked the lady, who had a badge with the name Sue Brown on it.

Tom decided it would be all right to nod as long as he didn't talk to the stranger.

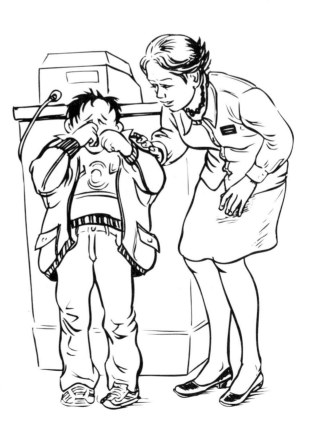

# LOST IN A SHOP (CONTINUED)

"Don't you worry, my dear," said Sue Brown. "You just stand there and I'll soon find your parents for you."

Tom did as he was told, but he couldn't help crying. He had never felt so alone or so afraid. Where could his parents be?

Suddenly, he looked up as a voice came over the loudspeakers which were placed around the shop. "Ladies and gentlemen, we have a little boy in the toy department who has lost his mother and father. He is wearing a blue coat and grey trousers. He is about five years old."

Tom was cross. "I'm not five, I'm six and I'm going to be seven next week!" he shouted.

"Yes, we know you are, Tom," said a voice which Tom knew very well. He turned around and saw his mother standing behind him.

"Where have you been?" cried Tom.

"We had a very special job to do," said Mrs Smith. "I'm so sorry that you were worried. We were only in another part of the shop and the lady at the till said she would keep an eye on you."

"What were you doing, Mum?" asked Tom as he dried his eyes.

"You'll find out on your birthday, my lad," said Mr Smith, who had just appeared.

Tom did find out what his parents' secret was when he opened his presents the next week. They had told him lots of times that they were sorry to have left him alone and he had forgiven them, but all the worry seemed worthwhile when he saw what they had bought for him.

# BAKING BREAD

## OBJECTIVES

| UNIT | SPELLING AND VOCABULARY | GRAMMAR AND PUNCTUATION | COMPREHENSION AND COMPOSITION |
|---|---|---|---|
| WRITING NON-FICTION 'Baking Bread'. | Collect and list time words. | Identify key words and phrases related to the language of time. | Use the language of time to structure a sequence of events. Write simple instructions. Use diagrams in instructions. |

## ORGANIZATION (3 HOURS)

| | INTRODUCTION | WHOLE-CLASS SKILLS WORK | DIFFERENTIATED GROUP ACTIVITIES | CONCLUSION |
|---|---|---|---|---|
| **HOUR 1** | Shared reading of 'Baking Bread' and discussion of time words. | Discuss new words and learn spellings. | 1: Re-read with expression. Prepare to read to an audience. 2*: Read and sequence text. 3: Explore words which help to structure a sequence of events. | Group 1 present their oral reading. Look at the text sequencing work done by Group 2. |
| **HOUR 2** | Shared re-reading of 'Baking Bread' and revision of time words. | Look at organizational devices for diagrams. | 1*: Explore words which help to structure a sequence of events. 2: Re-read with expression. Prepare to read to an audience. 3: Make a simple diagram to show how bread is made. | Look at Group 3's diagrams and prepare one on the board with the whole class. |
| **HOUR 3** | Re-reading of 'Baking Bread' and sequencing sentences. | Look at the spellings of time words. | 1*: Write instructions for making bread. 2: Make a simple diagram to show how bread is made. 3: Make a list of the instructions for making bread. | Read Group 1's instructions and discuss ways of improving them. |

## RESOURCES

Photocopiable pages 38 ('Baking Bread 1: Story'), 38 and 40 ('Baking Bread 2: The Wrong Order'), a list of sentences that describe a sequence of events but written in the wrong order (see 'Preparation' below), the word bank of directions/instruction words from the 'Right This Way' unit (page 22), board or flip chart, scissors, writing materials.

## PREPARATION

Make sufficient copies of photocopiable pages 38, 39 and 40 ('Baking Bread 1' and 'Baking Bread 2') for at least one between two. Write up on the board or a flip chart a sequence of events in the wrong order – for example:

> Finally, I went to bed and fell fast asleep.
> After that, I cleaned my teeth.
> At last, we reached the cottage by the sea.
> We set off at dawn.
> Last summer we went to stay in a cottage near some cliffs.
> After several hours wait, we set off again.
> Ten minutes after we set off, the car broke down.
> When we had unpacked, I drank a mug of tea.

Have ready the word bank produced in the 'Right This Way' unit on page 22 to show the whole class.

### Introduction and whole-class skills work

This unit has some similarities with the unit 'Right This Way' on directions and instructions which the children should already have experienced. Begin by asking them to recall the instructions and directions and show them a copy of the word bank which was produced.

Look at the story 'Baking Bread 1' (photocopiable page 38) with the children and ask them to listen to you reading it and to identify the words which signify a change in time. Re-read the text until they are able to pick out:

> *One day*
> *When I had finished*
> *Next*
> *Suddenly*
> *After doing that* and so on

Discuss the positioning of the words and phrases in the text. Draw the children's attention to the fact that the words and phrases which denote a change of time often appear at the beginning of a sentence or paragraph.

### Differentiated group activities

1: Ask this group to re-read the text with expression. Ask them to explore how the text is set out so that changes of time are often denoted by changes of paragraph. They should then prepare to read to an audience.

2*: Read photocopiable pages 39 and 40 ('Baking Bread 2'), where the story is set out in the wrong order. Discuss the most appropriate order for the sentences. You could ask the children to cut up the sentences and physically place them in the correct order, or they could write the sentences out on paper in the correct order. Some pairs of children from Group 2 could use the computer for this activity using cut and paste facilities to rearrange the text.

3: Ask the children to re-read the story 'Baking Bread 1' and to underline, highlight or write down the time words. When they have finished, they could try to think of further time words and write sentences which use them.

### Conclusion

Ask each group to tell the class about what they have been doing. Ask Group 1 to present their oral reading. Look at Group 2's work, highlighting points about key words, paragraphs and sequencing.

### Introduction and whole-class skills work

Begin by re-reading the story 'Baking Bread 1' and then ask the children to help you to pick out the key events. Show them how they could make a diagram (perhaps a flow chart or list with arrows) to present the events simply. Discuss the spellings of any unfamiliar words and add these to the word bank.

### Differentiated group activities

1*: Exercise on time words (as Group 3, Hour 1).

2: Ask this group to re-read the text with expression. They should then prepare to read to an audience.

3: Following on from the introductory session, ask the children to make simple diagrams to show how bread is made. Encourage the use of arrows and flow charts.

### Conclusion

Look at Group 3's diagrams and prepare a diagram on the board with the whole class based upon 'Baking Bread 1'. Discuss the organizational devices which could be used and show how arrows, lines, boxes and keys can be used to show a sequence of relationships.

### Introduction and whole-class skills work

Begin by discussing the importance of presenting instructions and stories in the correct order. Use a list of events which are presented in a non-chronological way to highlight this. Ask the children to help you to rearrange the sentences into the right order.

Look again at photocopiable pages 39 and 40 ('Baking Bread 2: The Wrong Order') and ask the children to use key words related to time to help you to find the correct order. Look in particular at 'after that', 'first' and 'finally' and ask the children what these words and phrases tell them about the order of sentences which begin with them.

### Differentiated group activities

1: Ask the children to write out a list of the instructions for making bread, encouraging them to discuss the text but ensuring that they do not merely copy it. Ask the children if they would like to add any instructions; they might wish, for instance, to be more precise about the mixing of the ingredients.

2: Make simple diagrams to show how bread is made (as Group 3, Hour 2).

3*: Ask the children to write out a list of the instructions for making bread, encouraging the use of time words. The children could use the diagrams which they made in the previous lesson and then elaborate by writing sentences, or the teacher could supply parts of the text on the board or flip chart and ask the children to complete it.

### Conclusion

Read aloud the instructions which Group 1 has produced and write some of them on the board. Discuss the instructions and ask children for suggestions for improving them. Ask Group 2 to read the text aloud to the rest of the class.

# BAKING BREAD 1: STORY

One day I decided that I would bake some bread. I did not have enough money to buy a loaf at the shop so I sat down and wrote out a list of all the things I would need.

When I had finished writing, I went to the kitchen and looked in the cupboards to see if I had the right ingredients.

First, I looked for flour. There was a big bag which was almost full.

Next, I looked for yeast. You need yeast when you make bread so that it will rise when you bake it. I found some yeast right at the back of one of the cupboards.

After a while, I looked in a recipe book to see if there was anything else which I would need. The only other ingredients were a pinch of salt and some water and I had plenty of both of those.

When I had all the ingredients ready, I mixed them in a bowl. When the ingredients were mixed, I began to knead the dough with my knuckles. You have to do this for a few minutes to make sure that the dough gets lots of air into it.

After doing that, I left the dough in a warm place next to the radiator so that it could begin to rise.

While I waited, I greased a baking tin and switched the oven on.

When the oven was hot and the dough had risen, I put the dough into the baking tin and put it into the oven.

After a few minutes, there was a wonderful smell of baking bread. I could hardly wait for the bread to be ready. I got out some jam and butter and a plate and knife and made a cup of tea while I waited.

Finally, it was time to take the bread out of the oven. The smell was fantastic. I took the loaf out of the tin and put it on a rack to cool. The bread was still warm when I cut the first slice. At last I could sit down and drink a cup of tea and eat bread and jam. It was lovely!

# BAKING BREAD 2: THE WRONG ORDER

■ Arrange the paragraphs into the right order.

After a few minutes, there was a wonderful smell of baking bread. I could hardly wait for the bread to be ready. I got out some jam and butter and a plate and knife and made a cup of tea while I waited.

Next, I looked for yeast. You need yeast when you make bread so that it will rise when you bake it. I found some yeast right at the back of one of the cupboards.

First, I looked for flour. There was a big bag which was almost full.

After a while, I looked in a recipe book to see if there was anything else which I would need. The only other ingredients were a pinch of salt and some water and I had plenty of both of those.

When I had finished writing, I went to the kitchen and looked in the cupboards to see if I had all the right ingredients.

# BAKING BREAD 2: THE WRONG ORDER
## (CONTINUED)

One day I decided that I would bake some bread. I did not have enough money to buy a loaf at the shop so I sat down and wrote out a list of all the things I would need.

When I had all the ingredients ready, I mixed them in a bowl. When the ingredients were mixed, I began to knead the dough with my knuckles. You have to do this for a few minutes to make sure that the dough gets lots of air into it.

Finally, it was time to take the bread out of the oven. The smell was fantastic. I took the loaf out of the tin and put it on a rack to cool. The bread was still warm when I cut the first slice. At last I could sit down and drink a cup of tea and eat bread and jam. It was lovely!

After doing that, I left the dough in a warm place next to the radiator so that it could begin to rise.

While I waited, I greased a baking tin and switched the oven on.

When the oven was hot and the dough had risen, I put the dough into the baking tin and put it into the oven.

# CHARLIE'S A GOOD BOY NOW!

## OBJECTIVES

| UNIT | SPELLING AND VOCABULARY | GRAMMAR AND PUNCTUATION | COMPREHENSION AND COMPOSITION |
|---|---|---|---|
| READING AND WRITING FICTION 'Charlie's A Good Boy Now!' | Make a word bank of words with the vowel phonemes from List 3 of the National Literacy Strategy – oo, ar, oy and ow. Learn to read and spell new words related to the story. | Predict words from preceding and surrounding words. | Use the context of reading as a cue to predict meanings of words and make sense of what they read. Understand time and sequential relationships in stories. Discuss reasons for events in stories linked to plot. Use story structure to write about own experiences in similar form. |

## ORGANIZATION (5 HOURS)

| INTRODUCTION | WHOLE-CLASS SKILLS WORK | DIFFERENTIATED GROUP ACTIVITIES | CONCLUSION |
|---|---|---|---|
| **HOUR 1** Shared reading of 'Charlie's a Good Boy Now!' and discussion of plot. | Look at spelling of new words related to story and create a word bank. | 1: Write an ending to the story. 2*: Guided reading of the story. 3: Complete cloze exercise using the story. | Discuss Group 1's stories and look at new vocabulary. |
| **HOUR 2** Shared re-reading of 'Charlie's a Good Boy Now!' and discussion of story ending. | Look at words which have been used and which may be needed for writing stories and completing sentences. Create a word bank. | 1: Continue to write an ending to the story. 2: Complete cloze exercise using the story. 3*: Guided reading of the story. | Look at sentences completed by Groups 1 and 3 and discuss prediction. Shared work on other sentences. |
| **HOUR 3** Shared re-reading of 'Charlie's a Good Boy Now!' and examination of words which include oo, ar, oy or ow. | Develop reading and phonological awareness of the vowel phonemes oo, ar, oy and ow. Show children how to play the phoneme game and discuss words used in it. | 1*: Guided reading of the story. Look for oo words. 2: Complete cloze exercise using oo, ar, oy or ow words. 3: Play the phoneme game and match oo. ar, oy or ow words. | Select pupils from each of the groups to read and present their work and discuss responses. Play the phoneme game as a class. |
| **HOUR 4** Shared re-reading of 'Charlie's a Good Boy Now' and continuation of the phoneme game. | Revise and build upon work done in Hour 3. | 1: Play the phoneme game and match oo. ar, oy or ow words. 2*: Guided reading of the story. Look for oo words. 3: Complete cloze exercise using oo, ar, oy or ow words. | Shared oral work with teacher using cards with words which include the vowel phonemes oo, ar, oy and ow. |
| **HOUR 5** Shared re-reading of 'Charlie's a Good Boy Now!' and extension of the phoneme game. | Look at additional words for the phoneme game. | 1: Writing sentences using oo, ar, oy or ow words. 2: Play the phoneme game and match oo. ar, oy or ow words . 3*: Guided reading of the story. Look for oo words. | Further shared oral work with teacher using cards with words which include the vowel phonemes oo, ar, oy and ow. |

### RESOURCES

Photocopiable pages 45 and 46 ('Charlie's a Good Boy Now!'), photocopiable page 47 ('Charlie's A Good Boy Now! – Fill in the Blanks'), photocopiable page 48 ('Oo, Ar, Oy and Ow'), photocopiable page 49 ('Words for Phonemes Game'), board or flip chart, card for making individual word cards, a dictionary, highlighter pens, Blu-Tack, writing materials.

### PREPARATION

Prepare sufficient copies of photocopiable pages 45, 46 and 47 for each child to have a copy. Enlarge a copy of the story (photocopiable page 43) to at least A3 size. Make word cards with the words on photocopiable page 49 (Words for Phonemes Game). Have ready plenty of plain paper for the children to write words on.

### Introduction and whole-class skills work

Read the story on photocopiable pages 45 and 46 ('Charlie's a Good Boy Now!') to the children and discuss it with them. Talk with them about the plot and about what they think might happen next. Write the title on the board or flip chart and ask them if it helps them to predict what kind of ending there might be.

The topic of bullying is often close to children's own experiences and it may be worth discussing this in more detail at another time. Explain that Group 1 will be writing an ending for the story and that they will need some help with vocabulary and spellings. With the class, create a word bank using words from 'Charlie's a Good Boy Now!' and any others which the children suggest (see 'How to make a word bank', page 10 of the Introduction).

### Differentiated group activities

1: This group will be writing an ending for the story for two lessons. Encourage the children to begin by planning what they will write and making some notes. They should prepare to read their notes to an audience.

2*: Read through the story again with the children. Talk with them about unfamiliar words and discuss the content of the story.

3: Give each child a copy of photocopiable page 47 ('Charlie's A Good Boy Now! – Fill in the Blanks') and ask them to use the original text to complete the sentences.

### Conclusion

Ask some children from Group 1 to read their stories (or notes) aloud. Discuss their ideas so far and look at any new vocabulary which may have been used.

### Introduction and whole-class skills work

Begin by re-reading the story with the children and then discuss again how it might end. Talk about words which the children use in their suggestions and write these on the board to create a word bank which the children who are writing an ending may use. Emphasize the need to look closely at the words and to focus upon the 'difficult' parts. Highlight those words which contain the vowel phonemes from List 3 of the National Literacy Strategy – 'oo', 'ar', 'oy' and 'ow' – and look with the children at the graphemes which represent them. Ask the children to help you put the words in alphabetical order and discuss how this should help them to find those they need quickly.

### Differentiated group activities

1: Continuation from previous lesson of story writing.
2: Cloze exercise (as Group 3, Hour 1).
3*: Guided reading (as Group 2, Hour 1).

### Conclusion

Look at the sentences which Groups 2 and 3 have completed in the cloze exercise over the two lessons and discuss them with the whole class. Write further sentences on the board or flip chart which are incomplete and talk about the way in which we can obtain clues about missing words by reading up to and beyond them.

## Introduction and whole-class skills work

Write the following words on the board or flip chart and discuss them with the children:

*good*        *March*        *boy*        *now*

The words are all taken from the high frequency word List 1 of the National Literacy Strategy. Talk with the children about the sounds which the graphemes 'oo', 'ar', 'oy' and 'ow' produce in the words. Ask the children to tell you any other words that they know which have similar sounds. If they suggest, for example, 'food', discuss with them the fact that the 'oo' in 'food' makes a different sound from the 'oo' in 'good'. (This may not be so distinctively different for some accents, particularly some Scottish accents).

Re-read the story 'Charlie's a Good Boy Now!' to the children and ask the children to listen for these vowel sounds. Show the children the enlarged copy of the story and read it with them, inviting them to put up their hands when they read an appropriate word. Make a collection of word cards for each of the sounds and include words which have the same sounds but different spellings. These should be used to emphasize that phonemes can be created using a range of graphemes. This may be a good opportunity to talk with the children about the 44 phonemes which exist in English and to encourage them to think about the different ways in which they might be written. This could also form the basis of an activity at home with parents.

Explain how the phonemes game is played. Turn all the cards face down and then ask children to take turns to choose two to turn over and say the words written on each. If the cards have matching phonemes, for example as in 'good' and 'took' the player keeps the cards as a 'trick'. If the cards do not match they should be turned face down again and the next person takes a turn to choose two cards. The game is over when all the cards have been matched and the winner is the person with the most 'tricks'.

## Differentiated group activities

1*: Give the children copies of the story (photocopiable pages 45 and 46) and ask them to find and highlight, or underline, words which include the phoneme 'oo' as in 'good'. Tell them that they should think about the sounds in the words and not just the spellings.

2: Give each child a copy of photocopiable page 48 (Oo, Ar, Oy and Ow) and ask them to compete the sentences. The missing words in their sentences should all be taken from the list at the top of the worksheet. If they complete all of the sentences they could go on to write their own sentences with missing words containing the vowel phonemes for friends to complete.

3: Continuation of the phonemes game (as whole-class activity, Hour 3). When all of the cards have been taken the children should write the pairs of words down and should look for other words in a dictionary which could go with the pairs to make sets of three or four.

## Conclusion

Ask each group to tell the rest of the class about the activities which they have taken part in. Focus upon Group 3 and show the class how the game is played. You could make some extra large word cards and secure them to the board with Blu-Tack and play the game briefly with the class.

## Introduction and whole-class skills work

Read the story once again and ask the children to look again for words which include the phonemes 'oo', 'ar', 'oy' and 'ow'. Show the children the cards for the phoneme game again and go through them one at a time helping the children to read the words. Give out some of the words and then ask children, one at a time, to hold their card up. Ask all the children who have a word with a similar phoneme to hold theirs up. Use the children's response to promote discussion about the sounds in the words and their spellings. Remind the children how to play the phoneme matching game.

## Differentiated group activities

1: Play the phoneme game (as Group 3, Hour 3).
2*: Guided reading of the story (as Group 1, Hour 3).
3: Complete cloze exercise (as Group 2, Hour 3).

### Conclusion

Use the cards from the phoneme game once again to enable you to check on the children's understanding of the correspondence between phonemes and graphemes. Write words on the board and say them aloud and ask children to hold up their card if it has the same sound. After a few minutes ask the children to exchange cards and continue the exercise.

**HOUR 5**

### Introduction and whole-class skills work

Once again the lesson should begin with shared reading of the story. This time ask the children to look carefully for words which could be added to the phoneme game. As they suggest words, write them down on card. You may wish to prepare most of the cards in advance and ask the children if they can find the words you found and some more. You may wish to include the following:

| | | | |
|---|---|---|---|
| *harder* | *brown* | *look* | *Charlotte* |
| *slowly* | *coward* | *loudly* | *arms* |

Some of the words in the story contain some of the graphemes which are being focused upon, but they are used to make different phonemes – for example, the 'ow' in 'snow', 'throw' and 'thrown'. There are also many instances of the phonemes being made by different graphemes – for example, house ('ow'), would ('oo'), enough ('oo'). If the children suggest these words they should be praised for their observation and the opportunity should be taken to show that sounds can be made in different ways. Reiterate the common alternatives for the 'oy' sound ('oi') and the 'ow' sound ('ou').

### Differentiated group activities

1: Ask the children to write sentences containing words with the vowel phonemes 'oo', 'ar', 'oy' and 'ow'. Use the cards from in the phonemes game but encourage them to think of other words.
2: Play the phoneme game (as Group 3, Hour 3).
3*: Guided reading of the story (as Group 1, Hour 3).

### Conclusion

During this final session, take the opportunity to check children's understanding of the correspondence (or lack of it) between phonemes and graphemes once again by using the cards from the phoneme game. Introduce some words which include the phonemes, but which the children may not have met during the series of lessons, and discuss the way in which the words are spelled.

# CHARLIE'S A GOOD BOY NOW!

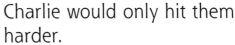

Everyone gave Charlie sweets. Some children even gave him their toys. No one ever said anything unkind to Charlie, but no one liked him.

No one ever called at Charlie's house to ask him to play. No one ever invited him to a birthday party or to tea, but almost everyone gave him presents.

Charlie was seven, but he was as tall as most children who were nine or even ten years old. He was much stronger than the other children and he knew it. If people did not give him their sweets and toys, he hit them or kicked them. Sometimes he twisted their arms or pinched them and no one dared to fight back or tell a teacher. They thought that if they did, Charlie would only hit them harder.

Then, one day in January, a new girl came to the school. Her name was Charlotte and she was easily the smallest person in the class. She had curly brown hair and big brown eyes and she seemed to smile and laugh all the time. The other children quickly became her friends and she always shared her toys at playtime.

One cold, snowy morning at playtime, Charlotte was admiring the snowman that she and her friends had just made. She was just about to bite into an apple when she felt a snowball crash into her face. The snow was cold and wet and she dropped her apple as she wiped it from her eyes and her cheeks. As she opened her eyes, she saw Charlie standing in front of her laughing and taking big bites from her apple.

"Ha ha, Charlotte's crying. Look everybody, Charlotte's crying!" he called.

# CHARLIE'S A GOOD BOY NOW! (CONTINUED)

Charlotte knew that Charlie had thrown the snowball and she was furious that he had stolen her apple, but she was not crying. "You are a coward, Charlie Walker!" she said very slowly, but loudly enough for everyone nearby to hear her. The children were suddenly silent. No-one had ever dared to call Charlie names before and now Charlotte, tiny Charlotte, had called him a coward.

"No I'm not!" shouted Charlie. "I can fight anyone in Year 2 or Year 3."

"Only because you're bigger than everyone else," said Charlotte. By now everyone was waiting for the awful moment when Charlie would hit or kick Charlotte.

"Someone get a teacher!" shouted Sunita.

"There's no need to do that," said Charlotte. "If Charlie wants to fight me he can, but it has to be a fair fight."

"What do you mean, a fair fight?" said Charlie who was getting very cross. He was not used to children who were willing to fight him. Usually, everyone just did as he told them to or he hit them.

"We'll have a snowball fight," said Charlotte. "Look, I'll stand over there next to that tree and you can stay here. We'll each make ten snowballs and whoever hits the other one the most times is the winner."

Charlie thought for a moment. He was much bigger than Charlotte and he was sure that he would be able to throw further. He would win easily. "All right," he said. "But don't go crying to the teacher when I cover you with snow."

"I won't if you won't," said Charlotte with a glint in her eye.

The other children stood back as Charlotte and Charlie began to prepare their snowballs. Some of Charlotte's friends tried to talk her out of the snowball fight. They didn't want her to get soaked and they were sure that she would lose.

# CHARLIE'S A GOOD BOY NOW!
# – FILL IN THE BLANKS

■ Complete the sentences.

No one _____ Charlie very much.

Charlie was _____ years old.

Charlie used to _____ the other children if they did not

give him _____ or toys.

A new girl called _____ came to Charlie's school in

_____ .

Charlotte was eating an _____ when a snowball hit her

in the _____ .

Charlie's last name was _____ .

Sunita shouted, "Someone get a _____ ."

Charlotte asked Charlie if he wanted a snowball _____ .

# OO, AR, OY AND OW

■ Fill in the gaps below from the words in the box above.

| | | | |
|---|---|---|---|
| boil | boys | car | cow |
| books | house | how | now | our |
| sound | too | toy | took |

Robert crept downstairs without making a _____ .

It was a bright, sunny day so Mrs Carter decided not to take the _____.

There was a lovely garden filled with flowers surrounding the _____.

Mr Kwan had four children, two girls and two _____ .

Sue went to the bookshop to buy some _____ .

Jack sold the _____ for a sack full of beans.

"_____ much does a bar of chocolate cost?" asked Simon.

Kahn put the kettle on to _____ some water.

# WORDS FOR PHONEMES GAME

| | | | |
|---|---|---|---|
| boil | boy | car | cow |
| good | how | soil | now |
| our | sound | took | toy |
| look | far | book | about |
| can't | good | four | pull |
| house | coin | jar | full |

# MONDAY'S CHILD

## OBJECTIVES

| UNIT | SPELLING AND VOCABULARY | GRAMMAR AND PUNCTUATION | COMPREHENSION AND COMPOSITION |
|---|---|---|---|
| READING POETRY 'Monday's Child'. | Read high frequency words on sight. | Revise knowledge of capitalization. | Use story structure to write an alphabetical story. |

## ORGANIZATION (1 HOUR)

| | INTRODUCTION | WHOLE-CLASS SKILLS WORK | DIFFERENTIATED GROUP ACTIVITIES | CONCLUSION |
|---|---|---|---|---|
| HOUR 1 | Shared reading of the rhyme 'Monday's Child'. | Look at the spellings of the days of the week. | 1: Use dictionaries to find words beginning with k, q, x and z and other letters suggested by the children. 2*: Guided reading of Catherine Storr's version of 'Monday's Child'. 3: Learn to spell the days of the week. Write out the rhyme for display. | Look at the spellings of the days of the week again. Ask Group 2 to read Catherine Storr's version of 'Monday's Child'. |

## RESOURCES

Photocopiable page 52 ('Monday's Child: 1'), photocopiable page 53 ('Monday's Child: 2'), dictionaries and other reference books, writing materials.

## PREPARATION

Prepare copies of photocopiable page 53 ('Monday's Child: 2') for every child and make an enlarged copy to at least A3 size. Prepare copies of photocopiable page 52 ('Monday's Child: 1') for Group 2.

### Introduction and whole-class skills work

Display an enlarged version of photocopiable page 54 (the traditional rhyme 'Monday's Child') and read it with the children. You will need to explain some of the vocabulary and, in particular, you may need to discuss the usage of the following:

> *fair of face*
> *full of grace*
> *full of woe*
> *Sabbath*
> *bonny and blithe and good and gay*

One way to illustrate what the words mean is to ask a child who was born on each day to come to the front and show them how to pose in a way which reflects their supposed attributes.

Help children to learn how to spell the days of the week. Show them that all the days end with 'day' so it is only the first part which they will need to learn. You may need to focus upon 'Wednesday' because it is not pronounced in quite the same way as it is spelled. Encourage the children to break it up and tell them that if they think of it as 'Wed-nes-day' and say it that way in their heads when they need to spell it they should get it right. They should, of course, say it in the conventional way for everyday usage.

## Differentiated group activities

1: Ask the children to use dictionaries and other reference books to look for words which begin with 'k', 'q', 'x' and 'z'. The children could also be asked to find words which begin with other letters for which there are few words in the high frequency list, or they could be encouraged to look for words which would help them to write their own version of 'Monday's Child' in a later lesson.

2*: Give each child a copy of photocopiable page 52 (Catherine Storr's version of the poem), read through it to them and help them to learn it. Discuss with them the differences between it and the original version and explain the vocabulary to them. In particular, you may need to help them with:

> *fairly*
> *tough*
> *tender*
> *enough*
> *roll*
> *casserole*
> *delicious*

3: Give each child a copy of photocopiable page 53 ('Monday's Child: 2') and ask them to learn how to spell the days of the week. Encourage them to work in pairs and to learn through the *Look, Say, Cover, Write, Check* method. Ask the children to copy the rhyme in their best handwriting for display. Tell them that they should begin new lines in the same places as in the rhyme and show them how to continue, with an indent, onto the next line when they run out of space.

## Conclusion

Look again at the spellings of the days of the week and hold an informal test. Ask Group 2 to read the alternative version of the poem aloud and ask the children which version they prefer and why.

# MONDAY'S CHILD: 1

Monday's child is fairly tough,
Tuesday's child is tender enough,
Wednesday's child is good to fry,
Thursday's child is best in pie.
Friday's child makes good meat roll,
Saturday's child is casserole.
But the child that is born on the Sabbath day,
Is delicious when eaten in any way.

*Catherine Storr*

# MONDAY'S CHILD: 2

Monday's child is fair of face,
Tuesday's child is full of grace,
Wednesday's child is full of woe,
Thursday's child has far to go,
Friday's child is loving and giving,
Saturday's child works hard for a living,
But the child that was born on the Sabbath day,
Is bonny and blithe and good and gay.

*Traditional*

# RHYMING LINES

## OBJECTIVES

| UNIT | SPELLING AND VOCABULARY | GRAMMAR AND PUNCTUATION | COMPREHENSION AND COMPOSITION |
|------|-------------------------|-------------------------|-------------------------------|
| READING AND WRITING POETRY 'Eight? Great!' and 'A dog called Dog' by Clive Riche. | Investigate and classify words with the same sounds some of which have different spellings. Make a collection of these words. | Understand that capital letters are needed at the beginnings of lines of poetry. Reorder sentences into a correct, logical sequence. | Read and write rhyming couplets. Write new lines for a poem. |

## ORGANIZATION (3 HOURS)

| | INTRODUCTION | WHOLE-CLASS SKILLS WORK | DIFFERENTIATED GROUP ACTIVITIES | CONCLUSION |
|---|-------------|------------------------|----------------------------------|------------|
| HOUR 1 | Shared reading of a short rhyming poem 'A dog called Dog'. | Raise phonological awareness of words with the same sound but different spellings. | 1*: Read and sequence text. 2: Re-read with expression. Prepare to read to an audience. 3: Create lists of rhyming words. | Select pupils from each of the groups to read and present their work. Discuss responses. Display new poems. |
| HOUR 2 | Shared reading of another short rhyming poem 'Eight? Great!'. | Raise phonological awareness by focusing upon rhyming words. Learn to spell numbers one to eight. | 1: Write another version of 'Eight? Great!' with different rhymes for each age. 2: Write the poem out. Re-read with expression. Prepare to read to an audience. 3*: Create lists of (different) rhyming words. | Select pupils from each of the groups to read and present their work. Discuss responses. Display new rhymes. |
| HOUR 3 | Shared re-reading of 'A dog called Dog' and 'Eight? Great!'. | Investigate words with the same sounds but different spellings. | 1: Write new lines for either of the two poems. 2: Sort words into rhyming sets. 3*: Guided reading of both poems. | Listen to lines written by Group 1. Look at rhyming sets produced by Group 2. Display new rhymes and lines. |

## RESOURCES

Photocopiable page 57 ('A dog called Dog'), photocopiable page 58 ('Eight? Great!'), a simple rhyming dictionary, board or flip chart, writing materials.

## PREPARATION

Enlarge Clive Riche's poems 'A dog called Dog' and 'Eight? Great!' to at least A3 size. Prepare sets of the individual lines of both poems on different pieces of paper.

### Introduction and whole-class skills work

Begin by reading the poem 'A dog called Dog' (photocopiable page 57) to the children and showing them the rhyme scheme, ask them to tell you about some of the less common words such as 'gambles', 'huffs', 'lugs', 'glumps' and 'snuzzles'.

Talk with them about the rhyming couplets and ask them to look for ones with similar and different spellings. For example, 'name' and 'game', 'dog' and 'bog', 'guzzles' and 'snuzzles' and 'sleep' and 'sheep' have similar spellings for the rhyming parts of the

V

Hosted by:

RM

# Riddles

| *Teaching Ideas > Literacy Ideas* | Subject: Literacy (English)<br>Age Range: 5 to 11 |
|---|---|

(The worksheet was contributed by Michele Papageorghiou)

Riddles are an ideal way to develop children's knowledge of rhyming. They are also great fun!

A worksheet which contains 7 riddles can be found <u>here</u>. Answers to these riddles are as follows:

This is a word which rhymes with cat,
It goes on your head because it's a HAT.

I'm useful for journeys when you're going far,
I need lots of petrol because I'm a CAR.

You'll find us near ponds or sitting on logs,
We jump and we croak because we are FROGS.

This is a word which rhymes with up.
You can drink out of me bcause I'm a CUP.

This is a word which rhymes with bake,
I'm nice to eat because I'm a CAKE.

This is a word which rhymes with spoon,
I shine at night because I'm the MOON.

A neverending circle, a bright shiny thing,
It's on my fourth finger because it's a RING.

When the children have worked out the answers to the riddles on the worksheet, they can easily try to make up some of their own. You could even make a riddles book, in which you can publish the children's riddles.

**Teaching Ideas**
http://www.teachingideas.co.uk
**Visit Teachers121!**
© **Mark Warner 1998-2002**

primary **MATHS** portfolio
Technology where it makes the biggest impact

words, but 'holes' and 'rolls' and 'barks' and 'parks' do not. Ask the children to think of other words which rhyme with some of the words, and write these on the board or flip chart. Talk about similar and different spellings as you do so.

### Differentiated group activities

1*: Provide the group with a set of the individual lines of the poem on separate pieces of paper and ask them first of all to match up the lines into couplets and then to put the poem into the correct order. If they finish early, they could try writing additional couplets for the poem. Some pairs of children from Group 1 could use the computer cut and paste facility for this activity.

2: Ask the children to write out the poem and learn it for presentation to the rest of the class. Encourage them to read with expression and to practise reading slowly and clearly so that their audience will enjoy the poem.

3: Ask the children to create their own lists of rhyming words similar to the one you wrote on the board. You may wish to provide a rhyming dictionary for the children to explore.

### Conclusion

Ask each group to tell the rest of the class about the work they have done. Look, in particular, at the lists which Group 3 made and write any new words on the board and discuss them with the class. Group 2 should have an opportunity to read the poem aloud.

### Introduction and whole-class skills work

Begin by reading the poem 'Eight? Great!' (photocopiable page 58) to the children and ask them if they can tell what the poet means by some of the clauses. For example, 'Hiding, playing peekaboo' probably refers to learning to walk. Ask them to re-read the poem with you and then ask them if they can think of other words which rhyme with each of the numbers. Write some numbers on the board and ask the children to contribute to a list of rhyming words for each.

For example:

| one | two | three | four |
|------|------|-------|------|
| gone | do | free | pour |
| none | glue | knee | door |

As part of the National Literacy Strategy List 1 of high frequency words, children are expected to learn to spell numbers one to twenty. Use the opportunity presented by the poem to teach the spellings of the numbers one to eight.

### Differentiated group activities

1: Ask the children to write their own version of 'Eight? Great!' with different rhymes for each age. Tell the children they may make use of the list of rhymes which you wrote on the board if they wish to, but encourage them to use others of their choice too. Talk with them about presentation and show them how the poem is set out and encourage them to present theirs in a similar way. Some pairs of children from Group 2 could use the computer for this activity.

2: Ask the children to write out the poem to help them learn it for presentation to the class. Encourage their presentational skills further by asking them to re-read the poem with expression and to practise reading slowly and clearly so that their audience will enjoy the poem.

3*: Ask the children to create their own lists of rhyming words similar to the one you wrote on the board You may wish to provide a rhyming dictionary for the children to explore.

### Conclusion

Ask each group to tell the rest of the class about some of the rhyming words which they have used. Where appropriate, add these to your list on the board and talk about the different ways in which the same phonemes may be spelled.

Ask Group 2 to read the poem 'Eight? Great!' aloud and ask Group 1 to read their own poems. Display these poems. This lesson could be developed into a series on the same theme.

### Introduction and whole-class skills work

Explain to the children that you are going to re-read to them the two poems which they have already met. After reading the poems, ask the children to talk about what they liked about each and encourage them to compare the ways in which each is presented. Talk with them about rhyming couplets and rhyming words and remind them of some of the rhymes they have seen before. Talk again about the ways in which the same sound can be represented by different letters and write some of the words on the board or flip chart and ask children to help you to match them where they rhyme. Mention in particular the vowel phonemes mentioned in the National Literacy Strategy list 3.

### Differentiated group activities

1: Ask the children to write new lines for either of the two poems. Ask them to choose their favourite and to write alternative or additional lines for it.

2: Provide this group with lines from both poems on separate sheets of paper and ask them to sort them first by poem and then into rhyming sets.

3*: Shared reading exercise: re-read the two poems which the children have met and look at any others which feature simple rhymes.

### Conclusion

Ask Group 1 to read aloud the lines they have written and make a note on the board of the rhyming words. Discuss their spelling with the children. Ask Group 2 to show their rhyming sets and add some to the list on the board. Talk again with the children about rhymes and about different spellings of the same sounds.

# A DOG CALLED DOG

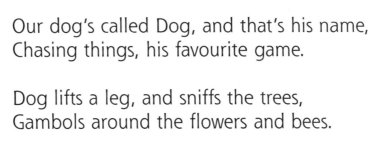

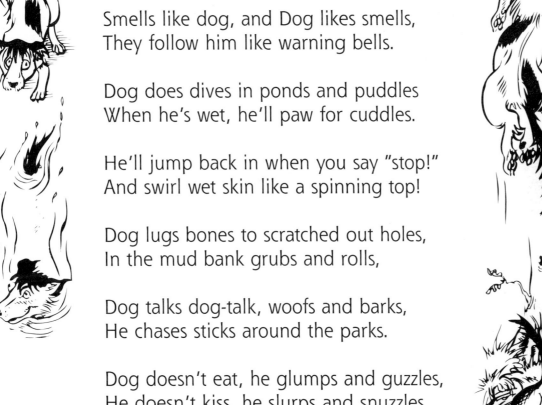

Our dog's called Dog, and that's his name,
Chasing things, his favourite game.

Dog lifts a leg, and sniffs the trees,
Gambols around the flowers and bees.

Smells like dog, and Dog likes smells,
They follow him like warning bells.

Dog does dives in ponds and puddles
When he's wet, he'll paw for cuddles.

He'll jump back in when you say "stop!"
And swirl wet skin like a spinning top!

Dog lugs bones to scratched out holes,
In the mud bank grubs and rolls,

Dog talks dog-talk, woofs and barks,
He chases sticks around the parks.

Dog doesn't eat, he glumps and guzzles,
He doesn't kiss, he slurps and snuzzles.

Dog, dog tired, goes to sleep,
He dreams of fat contented sheep.

In Doggy land, in distant shores.
Dog happy by the fireside...snores.

*Clive Riche*

# EIGHT? GREAT!

I WAS ONE
Not a baby but a son.

I WAS TWO
Hiding, playing peekaboo.

I WAS THREE
Growing tall just like a tree.

I WAS FOUR
Opening the big school door.

I WAS FIVE
Playing cars in the drive.

I WAS SIX
Telling time on the clock that
ticks.

I WAS SEVEN
Adding four to make eleven.

NOW I AM EIGHT
And I can skate.
Great!

*Clive Riche*

# AN ALPHABETICAL STORY

## OBJECTIVES

| UNIT | SPELLING AND VOCABULARY | GRAMMAR AND PUNCTUATION | COMPREHENSION AND COMPOSITION |
|------|--------------------------|--------------------------|-------------------------------|
| READING FICTION AND POETRY 'An Alphabetical Story'. | Read high frequency words on sight. | Revise knowledge of capitalization. | Use story structure to write an alphabetical story. |

## ORGANIZATION (2 HOURS)

| | INTRODUCTION | WHOLE-CLASS SKILLS WORK | DIFFERENTIATED GROUP ACTIVITIES | CONCLUSION |
|---|--------------|--------------------------|----------------------------------|------------|
| HOUR 1 | Shared reading of an alphabetical story. | Develop awareness of the spelling of high frequency words. | 1: Alphabetize words from the high frequency list. 2: Write sentences for an alphabetical story. 3*: Use dictionaries to find words beginning with *k, q, x* and *z*. | Select pupils from each of the groups to read and present their work. Discuss responses. Display new stories. |
| HOUR 2 | Shared writing of an alphabetical story. | Develop further awareness of the spelling of high frequency words. | 1: Write sentences for an alphabetical story. 2*: Use dictionaries to find words beginning with *k, q, x* and *z*, and other letters requested by the children. 3: Alphabetize words from the high frequency list. | Discuss high frequency words from List 1, especially those with irregular spellings. |

## RESOURCES

Photocopiable page 61 ('An Alphabetical Story'), a copy of the high frequency word List 1 from the National Literacy Strategy, individual cards with high frequency words written on them, dictionaries, other simple reference sources, board or flip chart, writing materials.

## PREPARATION

Enlarge copies of photocopiable page 61 to at least A3 size. Write the high frequency words shown in List 1 on individual cards. Have ready a collection of dictionaries and other reference sources.

### Introduction and whole-class skills work

Show the children an enlarged copy of photocopiable page 61 ('An Alphabetical Story') and read it aloud to them. Ask if anyone notices anything about the story. Ask the children if they can think of a sentence which begins with 'g' to continue the story. Draw their attention to the alphabetical list of high frequency words, but tell them that they may use other words too to begin sentences. Continue through the alphabet and write the sentences on the board or flip chart.

There are no words in the list which begin with 'k', 'q', 'x' or 'z' so you could ask the children if they can think of any. Encourage them to use dictionaries to do so and write their suggestions on the board. Tell them that one group will be given the job of finding words beginning with these letters to help the others.

### Differentiated group activities

1: Show the children the words from the list that have been written on individual pieces of card. Share the cards out so that each child has his or her own. Ask the children to place the words in alphabetical order. When individuals have done this with their cards they should put them together with those of a partner. Eventually, all the words should be placed in alphabetical order.

2: Ask the children to write sentences for a new alphabetical story. Encourage them to use the high frequency word list as a word bank and make use of words which the class has previously suggested for the letters 'k', 'q', 'x' and 'z'. Some pairs of children could use the computer to write their stories.

3*: Ask the children to use dictionaries and other reference books to find words which begin with 'k', 'q', 'x' and 'z'. The children could also be asked to find words which begin with other letters for which there are few words in the high frequency list.

### Conclusion

Ask each group to tell the rest of the class about the work they have done. Ask someone from Group 2 to read the alphabetical story aloud. Ask Group 3 to talk about the words they found and write these on the board or flip chart. Help the children to learn how to spell the words by segmenting them into phonemes.

### Introduction and whole-class skills work

Begin by reminding the children about the work they did in the previous lesson and then write a new alphabetical story together on the board or flip chart. Draw attention to the high frequency word list and discuss the words. Ask the children to read the words with you and use the individual word cards as flash cards to encourage sight reading.

### Differentiated group activities

1: Writing sentences for an alphabetical story (as Group 2, Hour 1).
2*: Dictionary exercise (as Group 3, Hour 1).
3: Alphabetizing activity (as Group 1, Hour 1).

### Conclusion

Use the plenary session to go through words from List 1. This is a good opportunity to focus upon those words which are irregular such as:

*laugh*
*love*
*once*
*one*
*people*
*their*
*two*
*who*

Draw particular attention to any words with which children have experienced problems and look at the structure of the words with the children.

# AN ALPHABETICAL STORY

After tea, Raj put on her coat and said
goodbye to her mother.

"Be careful, dear," called Mrs Singh.

"Can't you stop worrying about me?"
said Raj.

"Don't be late, Raj," said Mrs Singh.

"Every time I go to school you start to
worry," said Raj. "I'm going now!"

"First give me a kiss," said Mrs Singh
with a smile.

"Good...

"Have...

"I...

# GAME TIME

## OBJECTIVES

| UNIT | SPELLING AND VOCABULARY | GRAMMAR AND PUNCTUATION | COMPREHENSION AND COMPOSITION |
|------|-------------------------|-------------------------|-------------------------------|
| READING AND WRITING NON-FICTION Directions and instructions. | Spell words frequently used in instructions. Collect and list new words from reading. | Find examples in non-fiction of words and phrases that link sentences. | Explain in writing how to play a game. Read simple directions. |

## ORGANIZATION (5 HOURS)

| | INTRODUCTION | WHOLE-CLASS SKILLS WORK | DIFFERENTIATED GROUP ACTIVITIES | CONCLUSION |
|--|--------------|------------------------|--------------------------------|------------|
| HOUR 1 | Shared reading of a set of directions for a game. | Arrange sentences in a logical sequence. | 1: Write directions for a game. 2*: Read and sequence text. 3: Read rules for a game and fill in missing words. | Select pupils from each of the groups to read and present their work and discuss responses. Display directions for games. |
| HOUR 2 | Shared re-reading directions for a game and discussing ways of improving them. | Look at new words and create a word bank. | 1: Read and sequence text. 2: Read rules for a game and fill in missing words. 3*: Write directions for a game. | Look at directions written by Group 3 and discuss their clarity. |
| HOUR 3 | Shared reading of a piece of text with a set of instructions. | Develop reading by raising awareness of the way in which instructions are presented. | 1*: Read and sequence instructions. 2: Read text and follow instructions. 3: Read instructions and draw simple pictures which demonstrate understanding. | Select pupils from each of the groups and represent their work and discuss responses. Discuss key words and their structure. |
| HOUR 4 | Shared writing of instructions. | Look at key words needed for instructions and discuss spelling. | 1: Read text and follow instructions. 2: Read instructions and draw simple pictures which demonstrate understanding. 3*: Re-read and sequence instructions. | Discuss instructions and ask children to give instructions orally for simple tasks. |
| HOUR 5 | Shared writing of instructions with organizational devices. | Look at key words needed for instructions and discuss spelling. | 1: Writing instructions for an activity. 2*: Writing instructions with the teacher. 3: Make a list of key words for an activity and present them using organizational devices. | Discuss organizational devices used by Group 3. |

## RESOURCES

Sample sets of rules for games, photocopiable pages 66 and 67 ('The Rules for Playing Block'), photocopiable page 68 ('Making a Sandwich'), a set of sentences which are rules for a game produced on separate pieces of paper, a sample list of instructions (the photocopiable rules could be also be used for these two items, or a list of instructions from another source, such as self-assembly furniture), a set of incomplete rules, a set of instructions which are written in the wrong order such as photocopiable page 68 ('Making a Sandwich'), board or flip chart, scissors, drawing pins or Blu-Tack, highlighter pens, other writing materials.

Throughout the unit you should develop a word bank of words and phrases which are associated with instructions and directions (See 'How to make a word bank', page 10 of the Introduction).

## PREPARATION

Prepare copies of several sets of instructions – photocopiable pages 66 and 67 ('The Rules for Playing Block'), a set from another source (such as self-assembly furniture), one with the instructions in the wrong order (such as photocopiable page 68) and one with the instructions left incomplete. Write out the instructions for a game with each rule written on a separate sheet of paper.

**HOUR 1**

### Introduction and whole-class skills work

Ask the children to tell you about how they play a well-known game. This might be one which they have played in PE lessons or it could be one they play on the playground.

Show them the sample set of rules from the photocopiable pages 66 and 67 ('The Rules of Playing Block') and read through them slowly with the children. (The game has different names in different areas. The children may know it as 'Releasio', 'Ralico', 'Pom Pom' or by some other name.)

Next, cut up the rules and pin them onto the board (or affix with Blu-Tack) in a random order. Ask the children to look at the sentences carefully and then ask them to choose the one which should come first. When they have agreed on which this should be, move the sentence and place it at the top of the board. Now ask them which should come second and so on. Discuss with the children the ways in which some of the sentences begin with words which give clues as to their position. For example, a sentence beginning with 'next' could not be the first and a sentence beginning with 'finally' must be the last. Check against the original version of the rules.

### Differentiated group activities

1: Give this group the task of writing instructions for playing 'Hide and Seek' or another familiar game. Encourage them to begin sentences with appropriate words and provide a small word bank which includes words such as 'first', 'next', 'secondly' and 'finally'.
2*: Give this group a set of individual cards or pieces of paper on which are written rules for another game. Ask the children to physically rearrange the sentences to make a logical order for playing a game. When they have sorted out the order they should write the sentences out correctly. Some pairs of children could use the computer for this activity using cut and paste facilities to reorder the sentences correctly.
3: Give this group a set of rules for a game with some words missing. Ask them to read the sentences carefully and then insert the missing words. The final two rules should have only the first words of the sentences and the children should complete them.

### Conclusion

Ask someone from each group to tell the class about their activity and discuss with the children what they have learned about writing directions and instructions. Encourage them to try playing Block in the playground and at home and ask them to think about whether the instructions were clear. Display the directions the children have written.

### Introduction and whole-class skills work

Begin by asking if any of the children tried playing the game. Ask if they found the instructions clear and if they were able to explain them to others. Re-read the Rules for Playing Block (photocopiable pages 66 and 67) and ask the children to suggest any ways in which they could be improved or made more clear. Highlight any unfamiliar words and discuss their spellings. In particular, you may need to focus upon the following:

*touching*     *finished*     *person*     *captured*     *clockwise*     *direction*

Discuss the word 'block' and the associated words 'blocking' and 'blocked'. Add any new words to the word bank.

### Differentiated group activities

1: Reading and sequencing text activity (as Group 2, Hour 1).
2: Cloze (filling in missing words) test activity (as Group 3, Hour 1).
3*: Writing directions for a game (as Group 1, Hour 1).

### Conclusion

Ask members of Group 3 to read out the instructions for their games without revealing the names of the games. Ask the rest of the class to listen carefully and see if they can identify the games.

### Introduction and whole-class skills work

Talk with the children about an everyday activity with which they are all familiar. This could be getting dressed, cleaning teeth, making a sandwich or helping with a job at home. Show them a sample list of instructions for a task, but make sure that it is incomplete or in the wrong order or both. Photocopiable page 68 ('Making a Sandwich') could be used. Gauge the children's capabilities and decide what they will be able to understand. Read the instructions with them and ask them if they have any comments, such as: Are the instructions in the right order?

Ask the children if there are any instructions which they can tell straight away must come at the beginning or end. Discuss words such as 'finally' and 'first'. Ask them if they can find instructions which must follow other instructions – for example, 'Now sit down and enjoy your sandwich' must come after most of the other sentences.

### Differentiated group activities

1*: Give the children a set of instructions which are in the wrong order and ask them to read them carefully and then number them in the correct order. You could use photocopiable page 68 ('Making a Sandwich'). Ask them to write them down in the correct order if they have time. Encourage them to look for clues in the words and discuss again words like 'next', 'then' and 'finally'. Ask them if they can find any sentences which could easily be placed in different places (this applies to one sentence in particular on photocopiable page 68 – *You might like to put two kinds of filling in your sandwich. You could have cheese and tomato, tuna and cucumber or any other combination of things you like.*).

Pairs of children could use the computer for this activity using cut and paste facilities to rearrange the sentences.
2: Give the children a set of written instructions which they have to follow. For example, *'Write your name, write the name of your best friend, write the alphabet, write the name of your favourite food, draw a picture of a car...'.* Give them paper on which to follow the instructions. If they finish early, they could try writing some instructions of their own.
3: Give the children a set of simple instructions and ask them to draw simple pictures which could replace the instructions. You may like to show them samples from self-assembly furniture to give them ideas.

## Conclusion

Ask Group 1 to read out their instructions and invite the rest of the class to guess what the instructions were for. Groups 2 and 3 could read aloud their instructions and show their pictures. Discuss with the children some of the key words which they have used and write these on the board. Talk about the structure of the words and the graphemes which represent some of the phonemes. Focus, in particular, upon those which appear in the National Literacy Strategy List 3 ('oo', 'ar', 'oy' and 'ow').

## Introduction and whole-class skills work

Begin by re-reading the instructions for making a sandwich (photocopiable page 65) and then ask the children to choose another simple activity to produce instructions for. Use their ideas to draft instructions on the board and discuss, as you do so, letter formation, spellings and sentences structure.

Discuss the key words and phrases used in writing instructions and make a word bank of these. Include the following:

*first      next      after      that      finally      when      now*

## Differentiated group activities

1: Following instructions activity (as Group 2, Hour 3).
2: Drawing instructions in picture form activity (as Group 3, Hour 3).
3*: Reading and sequencing activity (as Group 1, Hour 3).

## Conclusion

Ask children to provide oral instructions for simple tasks, drawing upon the words which were discussed in the introductory session.

## Introduction and whole-class skills work

Begin by looking again at the instructions which you produced with the class during the previous lesson. If the words are on the board, erase all but the key words which denote a change of time or which were discussed in Hour 4. If the instructions were written in some other way, pick out and rewrite the key words and phrases. Now ask the children to use these key words as a framework for writing instructions for another activity. Discuss, and help the children to spell, any words which relate to instructions which they have not previously used.

## Differentiated group activities

1: Ask the group to write instructions for an activity of their choice. Encourage them to use the growing word bank of words and phrases which will have built up during the sequence of previous lessons.
2*: Writing instructions activity as Group 1, but with teacher support.
3: Ask the children to think of an activity and to make a list of key words which would need to appear in a set of instructions. Encourage the children to make an attempt at words which they are not sure how to spell. Ask the children to present the words in sequence, perhaps using arrows or numbers to show the order in which events take place.

## Conclusion

Discuss the work which Group 3 did in Hour 5 with the whole class, drawing attention to the organizational devices used. Make use of the children's attempts at spelling to teach the class some of the words which they have used. These could then be added to the word bank.

# THE RULES FOR PLAYING BLOCK

■ All of the players should hold out one hand each and stand in a circle facing each other.

■ One player should then begin to say a rhyme touching each player's hand in turn as he says each word. He or she should go around the players in a clockwise direction.

■ The player whose hand is touched on the last word of the rhyme is 'it'.

■ The player who is 'it' should cover his or her eyes and stand next to the blocking post and count to fifty.

■ All of the other players should hide.

■ When the person who is 'it' has finished counting, he or she should begin to look for the other players.

■ If the person who is 'it' sees another player, he or she should run back to the blocking post and shout 'Block 1, 2, 3' and the player's name.

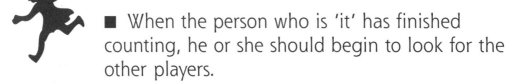

# THE RULES FOR PLAYING BLOCK
## (CONTINUED)

■ The player who has been seen and 'blocked' must stay next to the blocking post.

■ Then the person who is 'it' should try to find more players and 'block' them.

■ If any player gets to the blocking post without being seen by the person who is 'it', he or she can release all of the other players by shouting 'Block 1,2,3, save all!' The captured players may then go and hide again while the person who is 'it' counts to fifty again.

■ The game goes on until everyone has been seen and blocked by the person who is 'it'.

■ Finally, the first person to be captured has to be 'it' in the next game.

# MAKING A SANDWICH

■ Put the sentences in the correct order:

Now sit down and enjoy your sandwich.

Next take two slices of bread and butter each of them on one side only.

Place the other piece of bread, butter side down, on top of the filling.  If you do not want to use butter you could use margarine.

Finally, when you have finished, make sure that you clear away and wash your plate.

You might like to put two kinds of filling in your sandwich. You could have cheese and tomato, tuna and cucumber or any other combination of things you like.

First decide what kind of filling you would like in your sandwich and make sure that it is available.

Ask an adult if you may use a knife and then cut the sandwich into four equal pieces.

You could cut the sandwich into squares or triangles.

When you have buttered the bread, take the filling and place it on the buttered side of one slice of bread.

# CHLOE AND JACK

## OBJECTIVES

| UNIT | SPELLING AND VOCABULARY | GRAMMAR AND PUNCTUATION | COMPREHENSION AND COMPOSITION |
|---|---|---|---|
| READING FICTION 'Chloe and Jack'. | Understand and identify words which require capital letters. | Recognize and take account of capital letters and full stops to read aloud with appropriate expression. | Use grammatical cues to predict where punctuation should be placed. |

## ORGANIZATION (3 HOURS)

| | INTRODUCTION | WHOLE-CLASS SKILLS WORK | DIFFERENTIATED GROUP ACTIVITIES | CONCLUSION |
|---|---|---|---|---|
| **HOUR 1** | Shared reading of 'Chloe and Jack'. | Raise awareness of sentence punctuation. | 1: Write additional text which includes capitals and full stops.<br>2*: Guided reading of text. Identify punctuation.<br>3: Re-read with expression. Prepare to read to an audience. | Select pupils from each of the groups to read and present their work. Discuss responses. |
| **HOUR 2** | Shared re-reading of 'Chloe and Jack'. | Raise awareness of sentence punctuation, particularly capital letters. | 1: Re-read with expression. Prepare to read to an audience.<br>2: Write additional text which includes capitals and full stops.<br>3*: Guided reading of text. Identify punctuation. | Select pupils from each of the groups to read and present their work. Discuss responses. |
| **HOUR 3** | Shared re-reading of 'Chloe and Jack' with punctuation marks covered. | Identify punctuation in text. | 1: Write a short piece of prose. Cover punctuation marks to provide an exercise for the others.<br>2*: Guided reading of text. Discuss punctuation.<br>3: Write additional text which includes capital letters and full stops. | Look at Group 1's texts and undertake a brief assessment exercise. |

## RESOURCES

Photocopiable pages 72 ('Chloe and Jack: 1' – Punctuated) and 73 ('Chloe and Jack: 2' – Unpunctuated), enough identical copies of additional texts for Group 2 (possibly their reading books), Blu-Tack or Post-It notes, writing materials.

## PREPARATION

Make enlarged copies photocopiable pages 72 ('Chloe and Jack: 1' – Punctuation) and 73 ('Chloe and Jack: 2' – Unpunctuated). Make another enlarged copy of page 72 and cover the punctuation marks with Blu-Tack or Post-It notes.

**Note:** This unit focuses upon capital letters, commas and full stops, but other punctuation marks also appear in the texts. The extent to which these are discussed will depend upon your assessment of the children's readiness to be introduced to them. There is further work on punctuation, including speech marks, in the 'Jack and the Beanstalk' unit (see pages 143-148).

### Introduction and whole-class skills work

Read 'Chloe and Jack: 1' to the children and discuss the text with them. Display photocopiable page 73 (the unpunctuated version of the story) so that all of the children can see it, and ask one of them to read it aloud. The lack of punctuation will probably lead to the child finding this difficult, so do not let him or her continue all the way through the passage if this is the case.

Ask the child why it was difficult to read the text and discuss with the class the need for punctuation. Ask the children to look carefully at the text and to read it in their heads, trying to decide where full stops could be placed. If there is a volunteer willing to do so, ask a child to read the text and pause when he or she thinks there should be a full stop. Encourage discussion and invite others to offer their ideas.

Read the punctuated version of the text on photocopiable page 72 to the children, while they follow the unpunctuated version. Ask them to listen carefully and try to work out where the punctuation marks should be.

### Differentiated group activities

1: Ask the children to write an ending for the story and encourage them to include capital letters and full stops. Some pairs of children could use the computer for this activity.
2*: Talk with the children about full stops and commas and their purpose and encourage them to listen carefully to the text as you and they read it aloud.
3: Ask this group to re-read the text with expression. Ask them to look carefully at the unpunctuated text and to mark on it the places where they think they should pause. They should then prepare to read to an audience.

### Conclusion

Ask each group to tell the rest of the class about the work which they have done. Group 3 should have an opportunity to read the text aloud while the others follow. Encourage discussion about the punctuation which Groups 1 and 2 included.

### Introduction and whole-class skills work

This lesson is a development of the previous one and will provide more opportunities to discuss the use of capital letters. Show the children the piece of text with capital letters correctly placed (photocopiable page 72) and read it to them. Next, read through it again, but this time pause at each capital letter and ask the children to explain why a capital has been used. You might label each capital with an 'S' for the start of a sentence and an 'N' for a name.

Spend time writing examples of words on the board which always have capital letters. This may be an opportunity to draw attention to days of the week, months of the year and names and addresses which all appear in the high frequency word List 1 of the National Literacy Strategy.

## Differentiated group activities

1: Ask the children to re-read the original text, as well as the additional text they prepared during the previous lesson. Ask them to look carefully at the punctuation and capital letters. They should then prepare to read to an audience.
2: Writing additional text exercise (as Group 1, Hour 1).
3*: Guided reading activity (as Group 2, Hour 1).

## Conclusion

Ask each group to tell the rest of the class about the work which has been done. Group 1 should have an opportunity to read the text aloud while the others follow. Encourage discussion about the punctuation which Group 2 included.

## Introduction and whole-class skills work

For the final lesson in the series, you will need an enlarged copy of photocopiable page 72 ('Chloe and Jack: 1') with the punctuation marks covered by Blu-Tack or Post-It notes. The Blu-Tack (or Post-It notes) will show the children *where* the punctuation marks should be, but not *what* they should be. After re-reading the story with them talk about the ways in which they could be detectives looking for clues to help them to identify the punctuation. As you talk with the children, ask them questions such as:

> *How do you know that the punctuation mark before 'The' is a full stop and not a comma?*

> *What tells you that the punctuation mark after 'stopped' can't be a full stop?*

The questions should be designed to encourage children to look at the text around the punctuation and to use clues like the presence of capital letters and paragraphs to help them to identify punctuation marks.

## Differentiated group activities

1: Ask the children to write a short piece of text and to punctuate properly. Ask them to cover the punctuation with Blu-Tack (or Post-It notes) in the same way as you prepared the 'Chloe and Jack' story. This will then serve as an exercise for the rest of the class in the same way.
2*: Guided reading exercise. Ask the children to read another piece of text with you and discuss the punctuation in the text. The additional text prepared in the previous lesson may be used for this purpose, or the children's reading books may be used for this activity, provided there are sufficient copies for each child to have the same edition.
3: Ask the children to write some additional text which includes capital letters and full stops as an ending for the 'Chloe and Jack' story.

## Conclusion

Show the class the work which Group 1 have prepared and discuss the punctuation marks which they have covered. As this is the final lesson in the unit, it may be worthwhile assessing children's understanding of punctuation by providing a brief exercise for everyone to attempt. This could comprise a short, simple passage with no punctuation or capital letters which the children would have to correct. Ask the children in Group 3 to share their story endings.

# CHLOE AND JACK: 1

Chloe and Jack walked through the park. The sun was shining and birds were singing. Children were playing on swings and slides. A lady was selling ice cream from a brightly painted kiosk.

Suddenly, Chloe felt something wet on her arm. She looked down and saw a large black dog. Jack turned round and saw the dog too. Its coat was wet and it looked as if it had been swimming in the lake. It had a collar with a tag with its name on.

Chloe bent down and took hold of the tag. On it were written the words, "Sam, 7 Oak Road, Armthorpe".

The children decided to carry on walking. They had promised to be home by four o'clock and it was already ten minutes to. As they walked along the path through the park, Sam the dog followed them. Every time they stopped, they told him to go away and find his owner, but he took no notice. When they reached the park gates they tried once again to send Sam away, but he just looked at them with sad eyes.

Chloe and Jack did not know what to do. They had been followed home by a dog before and their father had not been very pleased. They had had to take the dog to the RSPCA because it had no collar and the dog had made a mess in the car on the way.

"What shall we do, Chloe?" asked Jack.

# CHLOE AND JACK: 2

chloe and jack walked through the park the sun was shining and birds were singing children were playing on swings and slides a lady was selling ice cream from a brightly painted kiosk

suddenly chloe felt something wet on her arm she looked down and saw a large black dog jack turned round and saw the dog too its coat was wet and it looked as if it had been swimming in the lake it had a collar with a tag with its name on

chloe bent down and took hold of the tag on it were written the words sam 7 oak road armthorpe

the children decided to carry on walking they had promised to be home by four o'clock and it was already ten minutes to as they walked along the path through the park sam the dog followed them every time they stopped they told him to go away and find his owner but he took no notice when they reached the park gates they tried once again to send sam away but he just looked at them with sad eyes

chloe and jack did not know what to do they had been followed home by a dog before and their father had not been very pleased they had had to take the dog to the rspca because it had no collar and the dog had made a mess in the car on the way

what shall we do chloe asked jack

# WHAT'S COOKING?

## OBJECTIVES

| UNIT | SPELLING AND VOCABULARY | GRAMMAR AND PUNCTUATION | COMPREHENSION AND COMPOSITION |
|------|-------------------------|-------------------------|-------------------------------|
| READING AND WRITING NON-FICTION. Recipes. | Collect and list new words from reading. | Understand how points can be listed and the sequential nature of directions. Focus upon the language of instruction. | Read simple directions for making things. Write simple directions for cooking using the appropriate register. |

## ORGANIZATION (2 HOURS)

| | INTRODUCTION | WHOLE-CLASS SKILLS WORK | DIFFERENTIATED GROUP ACTIVITIES | CONCLUSION |
|---|-------------|------------------------|--------------------------------|------------|
| **HOUR 1** | Shared reading of recipes. | Look at organizational devices in the language of instruction. | 1: Read recipes and list ingredients. 2*: Read and sequence text. 3: Read recipes and fill in missing words. | Select pupils from each group to read and present their work and discuss responses. Identify verbs in recipes as a class. |
| **HOUR 2** | Discussion of recipes and their layout. | Look at the vocabulary of instruction including phrases that link sentences. | 1*(first): Use a list of key words for writing a simple recipe. 2: Read recipes and fill in missing words. 3*(second): Read and sequence text. | Discuss recipes produced by Group 1 and examine the clarity of instructions. |

## RESOURCES

Photocopiable page 76 ('Scrambled Eggs'), some large and well-illustrated recipe books (especially any which are written specifically for children), a recipe with the list of ingredients removed, a recipe which has had key words removed, other sample recipes from books and magazines, board or flip chart, writing materials.

## PREPARATION

Make sufficient copies of photocopiable page 76 ('Scrambled Eggs') for each child to have one. Write out on the flip chart or board a list of key words likely to be encountered in recipes, leaving room for the children's suggestions to be added to the list. Enlarge a recipe from a book or magazine and cut the instructions into individual cards. (Provide at least three sets of these to allow for children finishing them early.) Display colourful examples of recipes from magazines.

### Introduction and whole-class skills work

Introduce the children to recipes by showing them examples in books and magazines and then an enlarged version. Discuss the need for precision in instructions and highlight some of the key words.

Talk about ways in which the recipes are set out and draw attention to the way in which directions are sequenced. Recipes tend to be written in a concise way and often each numbered instruction begins with a verb such as 'make', 'cook', 'preheat' or 'spread'. Talk about the numbers which are provided in recipes to guide the cook when measuring ingredients.

### Differentiated group activities

1: Provide each child with a copy of a recipe without the list of ingredients needed and ask them to read it carefully and to identify and write down the names of all the ingredients which are needed. When they have finished, ask them to look at the original list of ingredients and compare this with their own.

2*: Provide the children with the set of cards of individual instructions from a recipe. and ask them to rearrange the sentences in the correct order. Have some additional recipe sentences available for those who finish early.

3: Provide the children with copies of photocopiable page 76 ('Scrambled Eggs') and ask the children to choose appropriate verbs from those provided to complete each part of the recipe.

### Conclusion

Ask each group to tell the rest of the class about the work. Discuss in particular the verbs which are used in recipes. Read some recipes aloud and/or show the children an enlarged version of a recipe and ask them to identify the verbs. Display other examples of recipes.

### Introducion and whole-class skills work

Discuss with the children the recipes that have been displayed in the classroom. Talk about ways in which the text is set out and the key words which appear in them. Write a recipe on the flip chart or board for a simple dish such as beans on toast with the children's help. As you write, remind them that the sentences will often begin with the imperative form of verbs such as 'take', 'fry', 'melt' and 'mix'. Talk with them about some of the other ways in which the instructions could begin – such as with adverbs of time like 'next', 'after that' and 'finally'. Explain that such words are superfluous if the instructions in a recipe are numbered.

### Differentiated group activities

1*(first half of group session): Ask the children to suggest key words as a starting point for writing a simple recipe. Write out on a large sheet of paper (on the flip chart or the board) the key words which the children might use and ask them to write sentences which include them in their recipes.

2: Cloze exercise (as Group 3, Hour 1).

3*: (second half of group session): Text sequencing exercise (as Group 2, Hour 2).

### Conclusion

Ask the children who have written recipes with you in Group 1 to read them to the rest of the class. Discuss the vocabulary they have used and ask the other children to consider whether the instructions are clear. Ask members of Groups 2 and 3 to tell the rest of the class about ways in which they approached the sequencing and cloze exercises.

# SCRAMBLED EGGS

■ Fill in the blanks.

| take | beat | melt | pour |
| :---: | :---: | :---: | :---: |
| | stir | cooked | eat |

_____ two eggs and crack their shells.

_____ the eggs until they are well mixed.

_____ some butter in a pan.

_____ the eggs into the pan.

_____ the mixture as it cooks slowly.

When the eggs are _____ spoon them onto a plate.

_____ with toast and a grilled tomato.

# Term 2

# CHLOE CONFUSED

## OBJECTIVES

| UNIT | SPELLING AND VOCABULARY | GRAMMAR AND PUNCTUATION | COMPREHENSION AND COMPOSITION |
|---|---|---|---|
| READING FICTION 'Chloe Confused'. | Use phonic and word recognition. | Make use of punctuation to aid reading with expression. | Shared reading of a story. |

## ORGANIZATION (2 HOURS)

| | INTRODUCTION | WHOLE-CLASS SKILLS WORK | DIFFERENTIATED GROUP ACTIVITIES | CONCLUSION |
|---|---|---|---|---|
| HOUR 1 | Shared reading of 'Chloe Confused'. | Raise phonological awareness of the grapheme *ch*. | 1: Re-read with expression. Prepare to read to an audience. 2*: Read and identify words in text that include the grapheme *ch*. 3: Explore words that include the grapheme *ch* in the dictionary. | Select pupils from each of the group to read and present their work and discuss responses. Display collections of words that include the grapheme *ch*. |
| HOUR 2 | Shared re-reading of 'Chloe Confused'. Shared writing of a story. | Raise phonological awareness of the grapheme *ch*. | 1: Read and identify words in text that include the grapheme *ch*. 2: Explore words that include the grapheme *ch* in the dictionary. 3*: Explore real or invented words that include the grapheme *ch*. | Select pupils from each of the group to read and present their work and discuss responses. Display collections of words that include the grapheme *ch*. |

## RESOURCES

Photocopiable pages 80 and 81 ('Chloe Confused'), board or flip chart, dictionaries, paper, highlighter pens, pencils.

## PREPARATION

Make enough copies of photocopiable pages 80 and 81 ('Chloe Confused') for each child to have a copy of the story.

### Introduction and whole-class skills work

Write the grapheme 'ch' on the board and ask the children if any of them have that combination of letters in their names. Chloe is now a very popular girl's name. If you have a child called Chloe in the class, bring her out to the front and tell her that you are going to read a story about someone with the same name as her. Try to make use of other children's names too.

Read and show the story to the children and discuss the 'ch' words that appear in it. Ask them about other 'ch' words that they know. The story involves a trip to the shops where lots of 'ch' words with different sounds can be found. Can the children think of another 'ch' word that appears in the name of a shop (fish and chips, perhaps?).

Explain to the children that 'c' and 'h' often combine to make a 'ch' sound as in 'chips', but that they can also make a 'ck' sound as in 'chrome' or a 'sh' sound as in 'chef', 'charades' and 'Charlotte'.

### Differentiated group activities

1: Provide each child with a copy of the story and ask them to re-read it with expression. Ask them to look carefully at the punctuation as they read aloud and to work out a way of reading so that the 'ch' sounds are emphasized. They should then prepare to read to an audience.

2*: Provide each child with a copy of the story and ask them to re-read it. Ask them to find words that include the grapheme 'ch' and to underline or highlight them. Discuss the different phonemes it makes in different words.

3: Provide the group with enough dictionaries for one between two. Ask them to find words that begin with 'ch' and try to work out which particular sound each begins with. They could then produce lists under three headings: 'chip', 'chemist' and 'chef' so that they reinforce the idea that the 'ch' grapheme has different sounds.

### Conclusion

Ask each group to present its work to the class. Emphasize that 'ch' can be sounded in different ways and draw attention to some examples. Ask the children to make collections of 'ch' words at home and when they go shopping. Display a collection of 'ch' words.

### Introduction and whole-class skills work

Begin by discussing the 'ch' digraph and the different sounds which it can be used to make. Talk about the Chloe story and read it again, taking the opportunity to discuss any words that the children may find difficult to read. Tell the children that you are going to write another story together about Chloe and remind them that the grapheme has at least three phonemes. (You might like to make this a 'reading walk', too.) Write the story on the board with the children's help and make sure that they see and discuss the way in which you use punctuation and the way in which you form letters. Discuss spelling possibilities, particularly those that relate to 'ch'.

### Differentiated group activities

1: Reading exercise identifying 'ch' words (as Group 2, Hour 1).
2: Dictionary exercise (as Group 3, Hour 1).
3*: Ask the children to use the onset 'ch' and add rimes to make as many words as possible. They should write these down. The words could be invented or real. When they have finished, ask them to tell you how they would pronounce each word.

### Conclusion

Make use of the work done by Group 2 using dictionaries and produce a list of words that begin with 'ch' on the board. Add these to your class list. Discuss the structures of the words and the phoneme that is produced for each from the grapheme 'ch'. Look at some of the words produced by Group 3 and discuss which are real. Use a dictionary to check the words and discuss their pronunciation.

# CHLOE CONFUSED

Chloe was cross. She was very cross.

Charlie, who sat next to her at school, had told her that she could not say her name properly.

"You don't sound the beginning of your name with a c sound like in cat," he said. "You should sound it with a ch sound like in chat."

Chloe was cross. She was very cross. Mrs Chadwick, her teacher, had taught the children that c and h made a ch sound like the one in choose. Chloe had not liked to argue, but she knew her name should not have that ch sound at the beginning. It would sound silly. She tried saying Chloe with the ch sound from chat and it just came out sounding stupid.

Chloe was cross. She was very cross. She was cross with Mrs Chadwick for telling everyone that c and h made a ch sound like the one in cheese. She was cross with Charlie for teasing her about her name. She was cross with her parents for giving her a name that began with ch but did not sound like the ch in chocolate.

Chloe was cross when she came home and she told her parents why.

"Right," said her mother, "we're going for a walk!"

Before she had time to say that she was tired and hungry, Chloe found herself walking out of the house and into the street with her mother holding her hand.

"Where are we going?" asked Chloe.

"We're going for a reading walk," answered her mother, Mrs Chambers. "And here is the first place we're going to stop."

They were standing near the church. "What's that building called, Chloe?" asked Mrs Chambers.

"It's a church, of course," replied Chloe.

"And what sound does church begin with?"

"Ch, just like all the other words except my stupid name."

"Let's have a look at that sign," said Mrs Chambers pointing to a big red board in the churchyard. Chloe read it carefully. There were times of church services and the name of the chaplain. At the bottom were the words Choir Practice every Friday at 6pm. Chloe read the words carefully. At first she sounded the ch in choir like a ch in chap, but her mother helped her and she was soon able to pronounce the word properly.

# CHLOE CONFUSED (CONTINUED)

"But c and h make a ch sound like in chum," insisted Chloe.

Her mother pointed to the top of the sign and Chloe slowly read the words with her mother's help. "Saint Christopher's Church," she read.

"Now there's another name like yours with c and h making a c sound like the one in cot," said Mrs Chambers. "Come on, we're going to the shops."

They went to the butcher's shop and Mrs Chambers bought some pork chops. "C and h make ch in chops," she told her daughter.

They went to the chemist's. "C and h make ch in chemist," said Chloe, who was beginning to understand why her mother had taken her for a walk.

They went to the sweet shop to buy chocolate and they looked in the window of the pet shop where a chameleon sat lazily in an aquarium.

In the newsagent's window there was a poster telling people they could buy Christmas cards for half price.

At the florist's Mrs Chambers bought some chrysanthemums and then they walked back home. They stopped at the restaurant and looked at a sign in the window that said New Chef Needed. "That's chef beginning with a ch which makes a sh sound like the one in shops!" said Chloe, and they both began to laugh.

The next day, Chloe met Charlie at the school gates. "I've got something to show you," she said. "Look!"

Chloe pointed to the noticeboard next to the school gates. "What does that say?" she asked.

"St Christopher's Church of England School," read Charlie.

"Are you sure that's how you say it?" teased Chloe. "I thought c and h always made a ch sound like in chump!"

# SNEEZLES/WAITING AT THE WINDOW

## OBJECTIVES

| UNIT | SPELLING AND VOCABULARY | GRAMMAR AND PUNCTUATION | COMPREHENSION AND COMPOSITION |
|---|---|---|---|
| READING AND WRITING POETRY 'Sneezles' and 'Waiting at the Window'. | Read and spell words containing the digraphs *wh* and *ph*. Learn new words from reading. | Use awareness of grammar to decipher unfamiliar and invented words. Read aloud with intonation and expression. | Develop an understanding of the language of poetry. Use structures from poetry as a basis for writing. Recite a poem taking account of punctuation. |

## ORGANIZATION (2 HOURS)

| | INTRODUCTION | WHOLE-CLASS SKILLS WORK | DIFFERENTIATED GROUP ACTIVITIES | CONCLUSION |
|---|---|---|---|---|
| **HOUR 1** | Shared reading of 'Sneezles' by AA Milne. | Discussion about words that are unfamiliar to children and words beginning with the digraphs *wh* or *ph*. | 1*(second): Write a poem that includes words beginning with the digraphs *wh* or *ph*. 2: Make a word bank of words beginning with the digraphs *wh* or *ph*. 3*(first): Guided reading with expression. Prepare to read to an audience. | Groups 2 and 3 read to the rest of the class. Discussion about rhyming words. |
| **HOUR 2** | Shared reading of 'Waiting at the Window' by AA Milne. | Look at rhyming words. Identify phonemes. | 1: Find additional rhyming words. 2*(second): Guided reading with expression. Prepare to read to an audience. 3*(first): Write poems about raindrops. | Listen to Group 3 reading aloud and looking at words containing the digraphs *wh* and *ph*. Listen to Group 1's poems. |

## RESOURCES

Photocopiable page 85 ('Sneezles'), photocopiable page 86 ('Waiting at the Window'), dictionaries, the children's reading books, board or flip chart, writing materials.

## PREPARATION

Enlarge or make an OHT of the two photocopiable pages. Make sufficient copies of the poem for each child to have a copy.

### Introduction and whole-class skills work

Read the poem 'Sneezles' to the children and then discuss it with them. Talk with the children about poetry and use the word 'poet' to describe the author.

Ask the childen to tell you if they heard any words beginning with 'wh' and 'ph' in the poem, and discuss these. Then ask them if they noticed any unusual words and re-read it so that they may listen for these. Show the children the enlarged version of the poem and ask them to look for words with which they are unfamiliar and for words which seem to be made up. The poem includes some words which the children may not know (for example, 'examined', 'swellings', 'physicians', 'conditions', 'expounded' and 'certainly'). Encourage them to look at the words in context and talk with the class about what the words might mean. Discuss, in particular, the invented words which are based upon real words. These are:

*reazles     sneezles     pleazle     freezles     breezles*

Ask the children if they can tell you which words they are based upon and compare the spellings of the real and invented words. All are phonically regular, so there should be an opportunity to show the children that the same phonemes may be represented by different graphemes – for example, 'reazles' for 'reasons', 'snealzes' for 'sneezes'.

### Differentiated group activities
1*(second): Ask the children to write a poem that includes words beginning with 'wh' or 'ph'. Provide them with simple dictionaries and spend time with them discussing pronunciation and meanings when they have produced a selection of words. Provide beginnings for lines of their poems. You could ask them to set out 'wh' words down the side of the page and then complete a poem. For example, a question poem with words could be:

*Why does it always rain on sports day?*
*When will we have a sunny day to race on?*
*Where do all the clouds come from?*
*Who decided that sports day should always be rainy?*
*Why does it always rain on sports day?*

Some pairs of children from Group 1 could use the computer for this activity.
2: Ask the children to write down a collection of words that begin with 'wh' or 'ph'. Encourage them to use their reading books as well as a simple dictionary.
3*(first): Read the poem together and then encourage the children to read the poem independently and to prepare to read it to an audience.

### Conclusion
Ask each group to tell the rest of the class about their work. Make sure that Group 3 have an opportunity to read the poem aloud. Look with the children at the 'wh' and 'ph' words that have been found and write these on the board or flip chart. Ask Group 1 to share their poems. This lesson could be developed into a series of lessons based upon the same poem with groups exchanging activities. You may also wish to introduce other poems that include invented or adapted words.

### Introduction and whole-class skills work

Ask the children if they have ever sat and watched droplets of rain running down the window pane. Tell them that you would like to read a poem in which a child does this. Ask them to listen carefully to 'Waiting at the Window' and then ask them to tell you how the child describes the raindrops.

Show the children the poem and re-read it. Talk about the raindrops being given names and about the way in which AA Milne describes their progress down the pane, reinforcing the term 'poet'. Read the poem a third time and this time ask the children to help you with the rhymes. Do this by pausing before the last word of each of the second rhyming couplets and encourage the children to supply the missing word. Talk about rhymes and discuss the way that some words have different spellings and yet still rhyme. In this poem, examples are 'rain' and 'pane', 'see' and 'be', 'worst' and 'first', 'ooze' and 'lose', 'on' and 'John', 'pane' and 'again', 'enough' and 'fluff', and 'sun' and 'won'. Write the words on the board or flip chart and discuss the ways in which the same phonemes may be made by different graphemes.

### Differentiated group activities

1: Provide the children with dictionaries and their reading books and ask the children to find additional rhyming words for those that appear at the ends of the lines in the poem. Encourage them to go through the alphabet to explore possibilities.

2*(second): Provide the children with copies of the poem and ask them to re-read it with expression. They should then prepare to read to an audience. Tell them that you will be looking, in particular, for reading that takes punctuation into account and which is expressive.

3*(first): Ask the children to write a poem about raindrops, following the structure used by Milne but using their own words. Tell them that their poems need only be short and that you are looking for good descriptions and good use of rhyme. Help them to produce a poem with you acting as scribe and then ask them to look at it together and discuss ways of improving it. Some pairs of children from Group 3 could use the computer for this activity.

### Conclusion

Ask Group 2 to read the poem to the class and ask Group 3 to read aloud the poems that they have written with you. Discuss the rhyming words used in Group 3's poems, and those collected by Group 1. Display the poems and encourage children to read them and to make suggestions for developing them.

# SNEEZLES

Christopher Robin
Had wheezles
And sneezles,
They bundled him
Into
His bed.
They gave him what goes
With a cold in the nose,
And some more for a cold
In the head.
They wondered
If wheezles
Could turn
Into measles,
If sneezles
Would turn
Into mumps;
They examined his chest
For a rash,
And the rest
Of his body for swellings and lumps.
They sent for some doctors

In sneezles
And wheezles
To tell them what ought
To be done.
All sorts of conditions
Of famous physicians
Came hurrying round
At a run.
They all made a note
Of the state of his throat,
They asked if he suffered from thirst;
They asked if the sneezles
Came *after* the wheezles,
Or if the first sneezles
Came first.
They said "If you teazle
A sneezle
Or wheezle,
A measle
May easily grow.
But humour or pleazle
The wheezle
Or sneezle,
The measle
Will certainly go."
They expounded the reazles
For sneezles
And wheezles,
The manner of measles
When new.
They said "If he freezles
In draughts and in breezles,
Then PHTHEEZLES
May even ensue."

. . . .

Christopher Robin
Got up in the morning.
The sneezles had vanished away.
And the look in his eye
Seemed to say to the sky,
*"Now, how to amuse them to-day?"*

*AA Milne*

# WAITING AT THE WINDOW

These are my two drops of rain
Waiting on the window-pane.

I am waiting here to see
Which the winning one will be.

Both of them have different names.
One is John and one is James.

All the best and all the worst
Comes from which of them is first.

James had just begun to ooze.
He's the one I want to lose.

John is waiting to begin.
He's the one I want to win.

James is going slowly on.
Something sort of sticks to John.

John is moving off at last.
James is going pretty fast.

John is rushing down the pane.
James is going slow again.

James has met a sort of smear.
John is getting very near.

Is he going fast enough?
(James has found a piece of fluff.)

John has hurried quickly by.
(James was talking to a fly.)

John is there, and John has won!
Look! I told you! Here's the sun!

*AA Milne*

# MY SHADOW

## OBJECTIVES

| UNIT | SPELLING AND VOCABULARY | GRAMMAR AND PUNCTUATION | COMPREHENSION AND COMPOSITION |
|------|------------------------|-------------------------|-------------------------------|
| READING POETRY 'My Shadow'. | Make a collection of unfamiliar words. | Read own writing. Check for grammatical sense and accuracy. Predict from text. | Use structure from poems as a basis for writing. |

## ORGANIZATION (1 HOUR)

| INTRODUCTION | WHOLE-CLASS SKILLS WORK | DIFFERENTIATED GROUP ACTIVITIES | CONCLUSION |
|--------------|------------------------|--------------------------------|------------|
| **HOUR 1** Shared reading of 'My Shadow' by Robert Louis Stevenson. | Make a word bank of unfamiliar words. | 1*(first): Guided reading with expression. Prepare to write additional verses. 2*(second): Write an additional verse for the poem 'My Shadow'. 3: Cloze exercise using the poem 'My Shadow'. | Look with whole class at Group 3's prediction work. Groups 1 and 2 to read poems aloud. |

## RESOURCES

Photocopiable page 89 ('My Shadow'), photocopiable page 90 ('My Shadow' – Fill in the Blanks), writing materials.

## PREPARATION

Make enough copies of photocopiable page 89 ('My Shadow') for each child in Groups 1 and 2 to have one. Make enough copies of photocopiable page 90 ('My Shadow' – Fill in the Blanks) for each child in Group 3 to have one and make an enlarged copy of it for the whole class to refer to.

### Introduction and whole-class skills work

Talk with the children about shadows. Ask them when it is possible to see shadows and when it is not. Ask the children to listen to the poem 'My Shadow' and to tell you what the child in it understands, and perhaps does not understand, about shadows. Encourage the children to look at the enlarged version or OHT of the poem to find words and phrases which justify their views.

Talk with the children about some of the words which will probably be unfamiliar to them such as 'nursie', 'notion' and 'arrant'. Explain that the poem was written a long time ago and that some words which we now use were not known then while some that were used then are not used so often nowadays. Make a word bank (see 'How to make a word bank', page 10 of the Introduction) of these words. Discuss the way in which we can use the text to help us to read unfamiliar words and show the children how they can read beyond these words and make use of the rhyming scheme to work out what missing words might be.

### Differentiated group activities

1*(first): Provide each child with a copy of photocopiable page 89 and ask them to re-read the poem with expression. They should then prepare to write additional verses

(possibly during extended writing periods outside the literacy hour itself).
2*(second): Provide each child with a copy of the poem and ask them to write an additional verse for 'My Shadow'. Ask them to make notes for their ideas and bring them together with Group 1 to discuss the verses which both groups will be writing. Group 1 should then go on to work independently while you work with Group 2.
3: Provide the children with a copy of photocopiable page 90 ('My Shadow' – Fill in the Blanks). Ask them to fill in the blanks. Some pairs of children from Group 3 could use the computer for this activity if the poem is saved as a file. If the children find this task too difficult, you could write the missing words in random order on the board or flip chart for them to choose from.

### Conclusion

Ask children in Groups 1 and 2 to read aloud their additional verses for the poem. Show the class the incomplete version of the poem which Group 3 worked on and discuss the clues which enabled them to find the missing words. This lesson could be developed into a series with groups exchanging activities and writing original poems or pieces of descriptive prose about shadows.

# MY SHADOW

I have a little shadow that goes in and out with me,
And what can be the use of him is more than I can see.
He is very, very, like me from the heels up to the head;
And I see him jump before me, when I jump into my bed.

The funniest thing about him is the way he likes to grow —
Not at all like proper children, which is always very slow;
For he sometimes shoots up taller like an india-rubber ball,
And he sometimes gets so little that there's none of him at all.

He hasn't got a notion of how children ought to play,
And can only make a fool of me in every sort of way.
He stays so close beside me, he's a coward you can see;
I'd think shame to stick to nursie as that shadow sticks to me!

One morning, very early, before the sun was up,
I rose and found the shining dew on every buttercup;
But my lazy little shadow, like an arrant sleepy-head,
Had stayed at home behind me and was fast asleep in bed.

*Robert Louis Stevenson*

# MY SHADOW – FILL IN THE BLANKS

■ Fill in the blanks below.

I have a little shadow that goes in and out with me,

And _____ can be the use of him is more than I can see.

He is very, very, like me from the heels up to the _____;

And I see him jump before me, when I jump into my bed.

The funniest _____ about him is the way he likes to grow —

Not at all like _____, which is always very slow;

For he sometimes shoots up taller like an india-rubber ball,

And he _____ gets so little that there's none of him at all.

He hasn't got a _____ of how children ought to play,

And can only make a _____ of me in every sort of way.

He stays so close beside me, he's a _____ you can see;

I'd think shame to stick to nursie as that _____ sticks to me!

One _____, very early, before the sun was up,

I rose and found the shining _____ on every buttercup;

But my _____ little shadow, like an arrant sleepy-head,

Had stayed at _____ behind me and was fast asleep in bed.

*Robert Louis Stevenson*

# WORDS WITHIN WORDS

## OBJECTIVES

| UNIT | SPELLING AND VOCABULARY | GRAMMAR AND PUNCTUATION | COMPREHENSION AND COMPOSITION |
|------|------------------------|------------------------|------------------------------|
| READING AND WRITING FICTION AND POETRY 'Words Within Words'. | Split compound words into their component parts. | Use awareness of grammar to decipher unfamiliar words. Read aloud with intonation and expression appropriate to grammar and punctuation. | Use phonological, contextual and graphic knowledge when reading texts. Make a glossary of compound words. Write a story and discuss a poem. |

## ORGANIZATION (3 HOURS)

| | INTRODUCTION | WHOLE-CLASS SKILLS WORK | DIFFERENTIATED GROUP ACTIVITIES | CONCLUSION |
|---|-------------|------------------------|--------------------------------|------------|
| HOUR 1 | Shared reading of 'Words Within words'. | Discuss the features of compound words. | 1: Re-read with expression. Prepare to read to an audience. Make notes for a story. 2*: Identify compound words within texts. 3: Make compound words from component parts. | Read aloud and discuss compound words. |
| HOUR 2 | Shared reading of sentences which include compound words. | Examine the differences between compound and multisyllabic words. Identify compound words. | 1*: Write a continuation of the story using compound words. 2: Re-read with expression. Prepare to read to an audience. Make notes for a story. 3: Make a glossary of the compound words made during the previous lesson. | Discuss continuation of the story. Explore compound words. |
| HOUR 3 | Shared reading of and discussion about a poem. | Develop reading by raising awareness of compound words. | 1: Make a glossary of compound words. 2: Write a continuation of the story using compound words. 3*: Identify compound words within texts. | Read text aloud. Discuss glossaries of compound words. |

## RESOURCES

Photocopiable page 94 ('Words Within Words'), photocopiable page 95 (Compound Words), simple text which includes compound words written on card or the flip chart, a list of compound and multisyllabic words, a piece of text which includes compound words (from a newspaper or magazine), board or flip chart, dictionaries, newspaper, highlighter pens, writing materials. A copy of the poem 'Mirror' by Martyn Wiley and Ian McMillan (in Benson, G (ed), 1990, *this poem doesn't rhyme*, Puffin) may be useful.

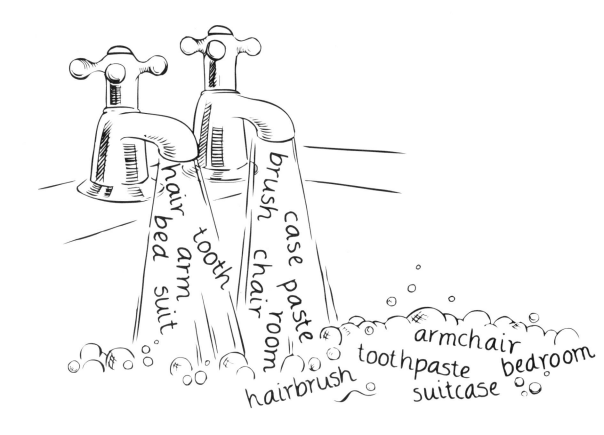

## PREPARATION

Make an enlarged version or OHT of photocopiable page 94 ('Words Within Words').
Make sufficient copies of photocopiable page 95 (Compound Words) for the whole class.
   **Note:** Compound words are formed by joining two words, the first of which identifies
a feature of the second. For example, 'postman' = a man who delivers the post,
'hairbrush' = a brush for hair. There is some inconsistency about the ways in which
compound words are written. Some are written as single words and some are
hyphenated. According to *Rediscover Grammar* (Crystal, 1988), once a compound
becomes established as a single word it tends to be written without a space or a hyphen.

### Introduction and whole-class skills work
Begin by reading photocopiable page 94 ('Words Within Words') to the children and
discussing it. Ask them to listen for some longer words and try to remember them and
then tell you what they were. Explain that some words are made by joining two words
together. After reading the text, ask the children to tell you the longer words they
spotted. Encourage them to pay attention to punctuation as they read, and to use the
context of the text to work out any unfamiliar text. As they do so, write the words on the
board or flip chart.

### Differentiated group activities
1: Ask this group to re-read the text with expression. Ask them to make notes on how
they would continue the story. They should then prepare to read to an audience.
2*: Provide the children with books or simple newspapers and ask them to spot and
write down as many compound words as possible together with their component parts.
For example, they might write 'football' = 'foot' + 'ball'.
3: Provide each child with a copy of photocopiable page 95 (Compound Words) and ask
them to make up as many compound words as possible and check these in a dictionary.
Explain that they may use words twice – for example, 'head' in 'headteacher' and
'headache'. Pairs of children from Group 3 could use the computer for this activity: the
children could use the cut and paste facility to create compound words and then use the
spellchecker to find out if the words exist.

### Conclusion

Ask each group to tell the rest of the class about the compound words they have found, and write some more examples on the board or flip chart. Ask Group 1 to read the story and tell the class about their ideas for continuing it.

### Introduction and whole-class skills work

Begin by showing the children, either on cards or on the board or flip chart, some sentences which include compound words and ask them to identify the words and their component parts. Next, show the children a list of words some of which are compound and some of which are multisyllabic but not compound. The words may be drawn from those produced by Group 3 in the previous lesson. Ask the children to identify the compound words and to take turns to come out and underline or highlight in different colours the words which combine to create them.

### Differentiated group activities

1*: Ask the children to use the notes which they made in the previous lesson to write a continuation of the story using some compound words. Encourage them to draw upon the compound words which have been discussed. Pairs of children from Group 1 could use the computer for this activity. The children should be encouraged to turn their notes into prose and to make use of the spellchecker as they draft their work.
2: Re-reading with expression exercise (as Group 1, Hour 1).
3: Ask the children to write a list of the compound words which they made in the previous lesson to create a glossary. Encourage them to look up definitions in the dictionaries.

### Conclusion

Read aloud and discuss some of the compound words and definitions which Group 3 created. Ask the children to look at the words as you write them on the board and to identify the words within them. Ask children from Group 1 to read aloud the stories they have written.

### Introduction and whole-class skills work

The children should, by this stage, all be familiar with compound words and should be aware that such words have particular qualities which are not shared by all multisyllablic words. Begin the lesson by reading a poem which includes some compound words to the children and discussing it. The poem 'Mirror' is thought-provoking and includes some compound words. Talk with the children about the poem and what it means and discuss the way in which it is set out and the fact that it does not rhyme. Only when the text has been discussed should the children be asked to identify the compound words.

### Differentiated group activities

1: Making compound words from component parts using photocopiable page 95 (Compound Words) (as Group 3, Hour 1).
2: Writing a continuation of the story (as Group 1, Hour 2). Encourage the children to draw upon the compound words which have been discussed.
3*: Identifying compound words within texts (as Group 2, Hour 1).

### Conclusion

Ask each group to tell the rest of the class about their work. Ask Group 2 to read their stories and Group 3 to show their glossaries. Invite all the children to suggest words which may be added to the glossaries.

# WORDS WITHIN WORDS

David put down his hairbrush and went to the bathroom. He picked up his toothbrush and squeezed some toothpaste onto the bristles.

As he was cleaning his teeth, he heard his father call that it was time for breakfast. He quickly put on his tracksuit and hurried to the bedroom. He could not find his sandshoes anywhere and so he went down to breakfast barefoot.

His older sister, Jill, was sitting in an armchair reading a newspaper. She was wearing a sweatshirt with the name of her favourite football team written on the front. Next to her, on the floor, was an eggcup and a teacup. Jill never sat at the table with the rest of the family. She said there was not enough room for her newspaper. The only time she ever sat at the table was when she was mending bits of her motorbike.

David sat down and poured himself some apple juice. At least, he tried to pour some juice but only managed to spill it all over the tablecloth. His grandfather, who was quietly drinking his tea, jumped up from his chair as he felt something wet dripping onto his feet.

"Sorry, Grandpa," said David as he mopped the juice up with a dishcloth.

Just at that moment they heard a huge crashing noise coming from outside the house. Everyone rushed to the window.

# COMPOUND WORDS

■ How many different compound words can you make using these words?  Write them below.

| | | | |
|---|---|---|---|
| foot | bag | hand | ball |
| post | lawn | man | mower |
| hair | dust | brush | bin |
| pan | sauce | suit | cross |
| case | road | book | head |
| ache | teacher | play | house | ground |

_____          _____

_____          _____

_____          _____

_____          _____

■ Can you think of any more?

I.M. MARSH LIBRARY LIVERPOOL L17 6BL
TEL 0151 231 5216/5299

# BEDTIME AND FOUR APPLES FALL

## OBJECTIVES

| UNIT | SPELLING AND VOCABULARY | GRAMMAR AND PUNCTUATION | COMPREHENSION AND COMPOSITION |
|---|---|---|---|
| READING FICTION AND POETRY 'Bedtime' and 'Four Apples Fall'. | Understand that some words have the same sounds but different spellings (homophones). Explore sets of words with different spellings of the same phoneme. | Use simple sentences to write a simple ending. | Read a poem and consider rhymes. Predict a story ending from an unfinished extract. |

## ORGANIZATION (2 HOURS)

| | INTRODUCTION | WHOLE-CLASS SKILLS WORK | DIFFERENTIATED GROUP ACTIVITIES | CONCLUSION |
|---|---|---|---|---|
| HOUR 1 | Shared reading of 'Bedtime' by Eleanor Farjeon. | Look at words containing the vowel phoneme or and discuss their spellings. | 1: Re-read with expression. Prepare to read to an audience. 2*: Read and identify words containing the vowel phoneme or. 3: Explore rhyming words and invent rhymes. | Group 1 to read poem to the rest of the class. Discussion about words containing the vowel phoneme or and their spellings. |
| HOUR 2 | Shared reading of 'Four Apples Fall'. Discussion about words containing the vowel phoneme or. Discussion about story endings. | Develop awareness of graphemes that produce the vowel phoneme or. | 1*: Read and identify words containing the vowel phoneme or. 2: Re-read text and write an ending to the story. 3: Explore simple story books to look at endings. | Select pupils from each of the groups to read and present their work. Discuss responses. |

## RESOURCES

The poem 'Bedtime', by Eleanor Farjeon (*The Oxford Treasury of Children's Poems*, ISBN 0-19-276134-X), photocopiable pages 99 and 100 ('Four Apples Fall'), a selection of story books, board or flip chart, highlighter pens, writing materials.

## PREPARATION

Make an enlarged copy or OHT of the poem 'Bedtime'. Make enough copies of photocopiable pages 99 and 100 for each child in Groups 1 and 2 to have one.

### Introduction and whole-class skills work

Read the poem 'Bedtime' by Eleanor Farjeon, to the children and ask them to listen to it carefully. Now tell them you are going to read it again, but this time you want them to listen especially for words with an 'or' sound. Ask them to put up their hands each time they hear a word containing the phoneme 'or'. Next, ask them to point to the 'or' words on the enlarged copy or OHT and write these on the board or highlight the parts of the words which have a grapheme to represent the phoneme 'or'. The words which the children should pick out are 'more', 'floor', 'four' and 'more' again.

Ask the children if they can think of any other words containing 'or'. As they suggest words, write them on the board underneath the words which have been found in the poem. The children will probably suggest some words which have other different spellings for 'or' and these might include 'awful', 'sauce' and 'ball'. Set the words out horizontally on the board and add new words suggested by the children to make lists. For example:

| floor | four | more | awful | sauce | ball |
|-------|------|------|-------|-------|------|
| door  | pour | sore | saw   | cause | fall |

### Differentiated group activities

1: Ask this group to re-read the poem 'Bedtime' with expression. Ask them to look out for words printed in italics and to emphasize these. They might try copying the poem out in their best handwriting, especially if this helps them to learn it. They should then prepare to read to an audience.

2*: Give each child a copy of photocopiable pages 99 and 100 ('Four Apples Fall') and ask them to read it and identify the words containing the vowel phoneme 'or'. Ask them to highlight these words or to write them down carefully. When they have finished, they might go on to make lists in the way that you showed them in the introductory session, adding new words which do not appear in the text. The text is designed to be used in follow-up lessons too. Some pairs of children from Group 2 could use the computer for this activity if the story is saved as a file.

3: Ensure that the children can see the list which you made on the board or flip chart of words containing the phoneme 'or'. Ask them to read the words carefully together and to pick out the graphemes which make an 'or' sound. They could go on to use the words at the ends of lines of short poems.

### Conclusion

Ask each group to tell the rest of the class what they have been doing. Refer back to the lists which you began on the board and ask the children from Groups 2 and 3 to help you to extend the lists longer. Ask the children from Group 1 to read the poem aloud to the others.

### Introduction and whole-class skills work

Begin by talking to the children about the previous lesson in which you looked at 'or' words in a poem and a story. Ask them to give you examples of 'or' words and write some of these on the board or flip chart. Only Group 2 saw the story 'Four Apples Fall' during the last lesson; this time Group 1 will be using it. Ask Group 2 to talk about the story and then read it to the class. Encourage them to listen for 'or' words and ask them to look for these as they follow.

Discuss story endings with the children and explain that some children will be looking at a selection of books to see how authors end their stories, while others will be writing their own endings for the story 'Four Apples Fall'. Ask the children to tell you some of the endings which they remember. These might be limited to 'They all lived happily ever after' in many cases, so you should have some alternative examples ready to show to the children.

### Differentiated group activities

1: Provide the children with copies of photocopiable pages 99 and 100 ('Four Apples Fall'). Ask them to underline or highlight the words containing the phoneme 'or' or to write them down carefully. When they have finished, they might go on to make lists in the way that you showed them previously, adding new words which do not appear in the text. Some pairs of children from Group 1 could use the computer for this activity if the text is saved as a file.

2: Provide the children with copies of the text 'Four Apples Fall' and ask them to read the story and try to work out a suitable ending to it. Children might work in pairs to do this. Encourage them to write at least four sentences for each pair.

3*: Provide the children with a selection of story books and ask them to look at the final pages to see how authors end their stories. Ask them to record the final sentences and then encourage them to discuss what they have found. Ask them if there are any common features.

### Conclusion

Ask each group to tell the rest of the class about what they have been doing. Encourage them to talk about story endings and show them some examples. Discuss the work done by Group 1 in order to reinforce knowledge of the vowel phoneme 'or'.

**Note:** The text 'Four Apples Fall' is designed to be used in follow-up lessons too. You could use it as the starting point for further prediction work, and it could also be used as a cloze exercise with the 'or' words removed and children being given a selection to choose from to fill in gaps.

# FOUR APPLES FALL

Paul was tall. In fact, he was very tall. He was so tall that he wore trousers with extra long legs. When he changed for PE, Paul took much more time than the other children. His clothes were so large that he had to use four desks to put them on, even when he had folded them four times.

When he played football, Paul was so tall that he always won the ball when it was in the air and he could head it for what seemed like miles.

Paul's sister, Dawn, was small. She had to stand on a chair if she wanted to see her brother's face. She had to call loudly to make him hear her when she wanted to talk to him, because his ears were so far from the ground.

One day, Paul and Dawn were picking apples in their garden. Actually, Paul picked them and then dropped them to Dawn who caught them and put them in a basket.

# FOUR APPLES FALL (CONTINUED)

Sometimes, when he picked an apple, Paul would accidentally shake the branches of the tree and other apples would fall to the ground. He always called to Dawn to warn her when an apple was about to fall and she would quickly get out of the way.

Unfortunately, Paul shook the tree too hard once and four apples began to fall all at once. "Look out Dawn!" he called, but it was too late. The apples bounced off her arms, her legs, her face and her back and she suddenly felt very sore.

"I"m not doing this any more, Paul!" she shouted and began to walk towards the house.

"Dawn, wait!" called Paul as Dawn reached the back door. "I"ve got an idea."

Dawn paused and turned to look at her brother. "It had better be a good one," she said. "My jaw is sore and I don't want to pick apples with you any more!"

# SYLLABLES

## OBJECTIVES

| UNIT | SPELLING AND VOCABULARY | GRAMMAR AND PUNCTUATION | COMPREHENSION AND COMPOSITION |
|---|---|---|---|
| READING FICTION AND POETRY Alphabetical and other lists. | Discriminate syllables orally and in writing. | Investigate other ways of presenting texts. | Identify features of sound in poems. |

## ORGANIZATION (2 HOURS)

| | INTRODUCTION | WHOLE-CLASS SKILLS WORK | DIFFERENTIATED GROUP ACTIVITIES | CONCLUSION |
|---|---|---|---|---|
| **HOUR 1** | Shared reading of a list of names. | Look at words and identify the number of syllables they contain. | 1: Read with expression. Prepare to read to an audience. 2*: Read text. Identify words with different numbers of syllables. 3: Use alphabetically ordered texts (such as dictionaries, indexes and listings) to find words with different numbers of syllables. | Discussion about multisyllabic words. |
| **HOUR 2** | Shared reading of a text. | Look at multisyllabic words. | 1: Sort lists of words into groups according to the number of syllables they contain. 2: Use alphabetically ordered texts (such as dictionaries, indexes and listings) to find words with different numbers of syllables. 3*: Read text. Identify words with different numbers of syllables. | Look at syllables in words from high frequency word List 1. |

## RESOURCES

A large list (at least A3) of the children's names, a large list of other multisyllabic words such as those found in the high frequency word List 1 (days of the week, months of the year and common colours), a list of other multisyllabic words (such as book titles, television programmes and place names), reading books or other pieces of prose, board or flip chart and pointer, writing materials.

## PREPARATION

Prepare enlarged copies of the list of children's names and the lists of other multisyllabic words. Make enough copies of the lists of multisyllabic words for each child in the class. Have the children's reading books and other pieces of prose ready.

### Introduction and whole-class skills work

Begin by showing the children an enlarged list of their first names. Ask children in turn to come to the front and point to names which you say. Read the list to them. Now tell them that you are going to clap some of the names. Clap the syllables (for example, one clap for Ann, two for David, three for Christopher). Ask the children to put up their hands if they think you have clapped their names. Explain that you are clapping the syllables and then ask them to take turns to clap their own names and say them as they do so. Encourage them to say the names slowly and to emphasize the syllable, for example, Chris-toph-er. If the children have understood what has been done so far, go on to clap first and last names and encourage the children to do the same.

Now try clapping the names of some of the children's favourite books and television programmes and ask them if they can guess the titles by counting the syllables. Write some of the titles on the board or flip chart and ask children to clap the words and then discuss the places where one syllable ends and another begins. Draw a line with coloured pen or chalk to show the boundary between the syllables.

### Differentiated group activities
1: Ask the group to read their books or any other prepared texts with expression. They should then prepare to read to the rest of the class. Ask the rest of the class to listen for multisyllabic words.

2*: Ask the children to read their books or any other prepared texts and to pick out words with different numbers of syllables. Ask them to choose one paragraph and make a list of all the single syllable, two-syllable, three-syllable and four-syllable words in it.

3: Provide the children with copies of any alphabetically ordered listings to find words with different numbers of syllables. The lists could comprise those which appear in the 'plus' section of List 1 of high frequency words – that is, days of the week, months, numbers to twenty, colours, pupils' names and addresses and the name and address of the school. Ask the children to make up questions for each other such as: *Can you find a two-syllable colour beginning with 'y'?*

Pairs of children from Group 3 could use the computer for this activity. Provide them with lists of words and ask them to sort them according to the number of syllables using the cut and paste facility.

### Conclusion
Ask each group to tell the rest of the class what they have been doing. Ask Group 3 to read out their questions and the rest of the class could look at enlarged lists and answer.

### Introduction and whole-class skills work
This second lesson on syllables should reinforce the work done in the previous lesson and should enable the children to consider different ways in which phonemes may be written.

Begin by making use of the writing in the classroom. Ask the children to look at displays and labels and pose questions such as: *I'm thinking of a two-syllable word beginning with 'c' which can be found in the kitchen* (cooker). As the children identify the words ask them to take turns to write them on the board. Ask the class to clap the syllables and discuss the ways in which the graphemes record the phonemes. Make particular use of words – such as 'scissors' – whose initial graphemes are less common. Talk to the children about other words with similar grapheme-phoneme correspondences ('science', 'scene', 'scent') and help them to learn to spell the words.

### Differentiated group activities
1: Provide each child with a list of names of children in the class and a list of other multisyllabic words (such as place names, book titles and television programmes) and ask them to sort them into groups according to the number of syllables each contains.

2: Find words with different numbers of syllables from alphabetically ordered listings (as Group 3, Hour 1).

3*: Identify words with different numbers of syllables from text (as Group 2, Hour 1).

### Conclusion
Bring the class together to discuss syllables. Ask each group to discuss the work which has been done and finish the lesson by drawing attention again to the lists of days, colours, months and so on, and clapping syllables for children to identify words.

# WHO AM I?

## OBJECTIVES

| UNIT | SPELLING AND VOCABULARY | GRAMMAR AND PUNCTUATION | COMPREHENSION AND COMPOSITION |
|---|---|---|---|
| READING AND WRITING FICTION 'Who am I?' | Segment words into phonemes for spelling. | Identify speech marks in reading. Understand their purpose and use terms correctly. | Prepare and re-tell stories through role play in groups using dialogue and narrative from text. |

## ORGANIZATION (3 HOURS)

| | INTRODUCTION | WHOLE-CLASS SKILLS WORK | DIFFERENTIATED GROUP ACTIVITIES | CONCLUSION |
|---|---|---|---|---|
| HOUR 1 | Shared reading and reading aloud of 'Who am I?' Discussion about speech marks. | Look at unfamiliar words. Segment them into phonemes to learn spellings. | 1: Write a dialogue. 2*: Guided reading of dialogue. 3: Identify spoken text. | Write out some of the dialogue produced by Group 1. Discuss the way it is presented. |
| HOUR 2 | Re-reading of 'Who am I?' Ask children to take the parts of various characters. | Look at the spelling of alternatives to *said* in dialogue. | 1*: Guided reading of dialogue. 2: Write a dialogue. 3: Find alternatives to *said* in reading books. | Compile a list of alternatives to *said* in dialogue. Look at spellings. |
| HOUR 3 | Identify speech in text. | Use punctuation marks. | 1: Write dialogue based upon cartoon strips. 2: Write dialogue based upon a conversation. 3*: Guided reading focusing upon speech marks. | Use cards to make up sentences that include speech marks. |

## RESOURCES

Photocopiable pages 106 and 107 ('Who am I?'), a list of words taken from List 1 in the National Literacy Strategy, a large set of word cards (some to be written on, some to remain blank), a selection of simple cartoon strips that include speech in bubbles, reading books, a simple text that includes dialogue, reading books, board or flip chart, highlighter pens, writing materials.

## PREPARATION

Make enough copies of photocopiable pages 106 and 107 ('Who am I?') for each child to have one. Make an enlarged copy or OHT of photocopiable pages 106 and 107. Prepare copies of another simple piece of text containing dialogue which the children can read in role play. Make a set of individual word cards on which you have written each of the children's names. Make a set of cards with words from List 1. Make a further set of cards on which you have written speech marks, commas, full stops, exclamation marks and question marks and, finally, make a set of cards of other words that the children have used recently.

Prepare copies of simple cartoon strips in which the characters' speech bubbles have been blanked out. Prepare a set of blank cards for writing words suggested by the children on. Have ready the children's reading books, and plenty of paper and writing materials.

### Introduction and whole-class skills work

Read aloud the text on photocopiable pages 106 and 107 ('Who Am I?') and then read it with the children. Ask the children to look at the first section of dialogue and then ask them questions such as:

*What did James say first?*
*What was Sasha's reply?*
*What did James ask Becky?*

Ask the children to tell you the exact words which were spoken and encourage them to identify the speech marks and discuss their usage.

The text includes some words with which children may not be familiar. Look at these with them and break them down into phonemes. The children's names are all phonically regular and may be a good starting point. Other words upon which you may need to focus include:

| | | |
|---|---|---|
| *famous* | *pinned* | *questions* |
| *answered* | *replied* | *television* |
| *usually* | *person* | *female* |
| *actress* | *cartoon* | *Peru* |
| *puppet* | *marmalade* | *character* |
| *twinkle* | *guessed* | |

### Differentiated group activities

1: Ask this group to write a dialogue for finding out which name was on Becky's back. Encourage them to think of a famous person and to make up appropriate questions. They could do this in pairs with one child writing Becky's words and the other writing answers to Becky's questions. Some pairs of children from Group 1 could use the computer for this activity.

2*: Provide the children with copies of photocopiable pages 106 and 107 ('Who am I?') and ask them to re-read the text with different children reading dialogue for different characters. Give an opportunity to all children to read some of the text – someone might read all the text around the speech while someone else could read the introductory paragraph.

3: Provide this group with copies of photocopiable pages 106 and 107 ('Who Am I?') and ask them to underline or highlight spoken text. Those who complete this activity could go on to look for further examples of dialogue in reading books.

### Conclusion

Ask Group 1 to read aloud examples of the dialogue that they have written. Write some of these on the board or flip chart with the help of the rest of the class. Pay particular attention to speech marks and show the children how dialogue is set out with each new speaker's words beginning on a new line.

### Introduction and whole-class skills work

Read 'Who Am I?' (on pages 106 and 107) to the children again and then choose four children to play the parts of the four in the text. Explain that the children are going to help you to read the text by saying the words which the children say. Talk with the children about what they will need to look out for to show them which words to say and which to let you say.

Some children, inevitably, will read straight through the speech marks. Use this as an opportunity to draw attention to the punctuation and allow children to attempt to re-read the text taking it into account. Draw attention to the words which denote how the speaker spoke and write these on the board or flip chart and discuss their spellings.

### Differentiated group activities

1*: Guided reading of dialogue (as Group 2, Hour 1).
2: Write a dialogue for finding out which name was on Dean's back (as Group 2, Hour 1). Some children could use the computer for this activity.
3: Ask the children to find alternatives to the word 'said' in their reading books. Explain

that they will need to find examples of dialogue and then to identify the verbs which are used to show how the speaker delivered the lines. The children may need to be given examples as a starting point. These could include:

| | | | |
|---|---|---|---|
| *answered* | *asked* | *replied* | *shouted* |
| *cried* | *laughed* | *whispered* | *muttered* |

### Conclusion
Ask Group 3 to help you to compile a list of alternative words to using 'said' in dialogue. Invite other children to make suggestions and to find examples from their reading books. List the words on the board and show the children how they are spelled.

### Introduction and whole-class skills work
Show the class an enlarged copy or OHT of any text that contains dialogue and ask the children to read it with you. Re-read the text, but assign the roles of different characters to different children or groups of children and ask them to read the dialogue. Discuss the use of punctuation marks and ask children to point them out.

Give each child a word card from those words which appear on List 1 or other frequently used words. Each child should also have a card with his or her name on it. In addition, you will need to choose some children to have cards with speech marks, commas, full stops, question marks and exclamation marks written on them.

Ask the children to look at their words and to read them. Choose a child to come to the front and hold up his or her name card. Ask the other children to choose a speech verb from the list compiled during the previous lesson, write this on a blank card and give it to the child to hold next to his or her name. Read the words with the children and then ask them for suggestions as to what the words spoken might be. Ask them to read the speech word in an appropriate way – for example, murmured, whispered, and so on. Ask children who hold the chosen words to come to the front and hold them up and arrange themselves into the right order. If a word is chosen which no one has yet picked, you could make an additional card showing the children how to spell the word, or you could ask the children to think of a suitable alternative.

When the sentence has been created, ask the children with punctuation cards to stand in the right place in the line of children to show where speech begins and ends. Invite the others to help them and to say where other punctuation marks could be placed. Repeat the exercise as many times as necessary, possibly asking children to exchange word and punctuation cards.

### Differentiated group activities
1: Provide this group with copies of simple cartoon strips and ask them to rewrite the text which appears in speech bubbles using speech marks and other text to say who was speaking and how they were saying it.
2: Ask this group to write a dialogue based upon a conversation between two people. Invite them to choose any two people they would like to write about. They might include themselves and a celebrity. Some pairs of children from Group 2 could use the computer for this activity.
3*: Guided reading of dialogue (as Group 2, Hour 1). The text could be 'Who am I?' or any other suitable text.

### Conclusion
Distribute the word and punctuation cards again and ask children to make up more sentences with dialogue. Use this final lesson of the series to assess whether children have understood the purpose of speech marks by asking them questions such as:

*Where do we put the first speech marks?*
*Where do we put the final speech marks?*
*How do we know when someone is speaking in a story we are reading?*

# WHO AM I?

James, Sasha, Becky and Dean were playing a game called Who Am I? Sasha's mother had written the names of four famous people on large pieces of paper and had pinned them to the back of each child's T-shirt. Everyone could see the name of everyone else, but no one knew which name was pinned to his or her own back. The idea of the game was for the children to ask each other questions and try to find out which names were pinned to their backs.

James began. "Am I male?" he asked Sasha.

"Yes, you are male," answered Sasha.

"Am I a sportsman?" he asked Becky.

"No, you're not a sportsman," she replied.

"Dean, can you tell me if I am ever on television please?" asked James.

"Yes, you are," said Dean, "but usually you are in films."

"Am I an actor, Sasha?" asked James.

"Sort of," said Sasha. "You are not a real person."

James thought about this. "Do you mean I'm someone like Batman?"

"Yes, you are someone like Batman, but you are not Batman," replied Sasha.

# WHO AM I? (CONTINUED)

"Am I Superman, Becky?" asked James.

"Yes, you are!" said Becky. "I bet you used your Superman powers to read the name on your back!" Everyone laughed.

Now it was Sasha's turn. The name on her back was Paddington Bear.

"Am I female?" Sasha asked James.

"No, you are a male," answered James.

"Am I an actor, Becky?" asked Sasha.

"No, but you have been on television and an actor says your words," replied Becky.

"Am I a cartoon character?" asked Sasha.

"Not really," replied Becky.

Sasha had an idea.

"James, am I an animal?" she asked.

"Yes, you are, but you're not a real animal," said James.

"Am I a puppet then?" asked Sasha.

"Sort of," said James smiling.

"Do I like marmalade sandwiches?" asked Sasha with a twinkle in her eye.

"I think you've guessed who you are!" laughed Becky.

"I'm Paddington Bear," said Sasha. "I'm from Darkest Peru!"

# THE RESCUE

## OBJECTIVES

| UNIT | SPELLING AND VOCABULARY | GRAMMAR AND PUNCTUATION | COMPREHENSION AND COMPOSITION |
|------|------------------------|------------------------|------------------------------|
| READING POETRY 'The Rescue'. | Create a word bank of rhyming words. Classify words with the same sounds but different spellings. | Identify key words and phrases. | Raise awareness of differences between story and poetic language. |

## ORGANIZATION (1 HOUR)

| | INTRODUCTION | WHOLE-CLASS SKILLS WORK | DIFFERENTIATED GROUP ACTIVITIES | CONCLUSION |
|---|------------|----------------------|-------------------------------|-----------|
| **HOUR 1** | Shared reading of 'The Rescue' by Ian Serraillier. | Raise phonological awareness by looking at rhyming words. | 1: Read and identify rhyming words in text. 2*(second): Explore rhyming words. Create a word bank of rhyming words. 3*(first): Guided reading with expression. Prepare to read to an audience. | Select pupils from each of the groups to read and present their work. Discuss responses. Display word banks of rhyming words and invite children to make additions. |

## RESOURCES

Photocopiable page 110 ('The Rescue' by Ian Serraillier), paper, writing materials.

## PREPARATION

Make enough copies of photocopiable page 110 for the children in Groups 1 and 3 to have a copy. Make an enlarged version or OHT of the poem.

### Introduction and whole-class skills work

Read the poem 'The Rescue' by Ian Serraillier from photocopiable page 110. Let the children follow on an enlarged copy or OHT as you read and then ask them to think about the devices which Serraillier uses to make the poem exciting (the sentences are short; he makes use of repetition and questions). Talk with them about the rhyming words and ask them to look carefully and try to identify them.

Re-read the poem to the children and ask them to listen for the rhymes. Discuss with the children the way in which the poet repeats some lines at the ends of verses. There is still a rhyme in these lines, but the words are the same. Ask the children why they think Ian Seraillier did this.

### Differentiated group activities

1: Give each child a copy of photocopiable page 110 and ask them to re-read the poem and to identify rhyming words within the text. Ask them to make a note of the pairs of rhyming words. They might add further rhyming words of their own choice if they finish early.

2*(second): Ask the children to compile a list of the rhyming words from 'The Rescue' and then invite them to write next to each word as many other words which rhyme with it as they can. Discuss spellings with them and talk, in particular, about the ways in which the same phoneme can often be represented by different graphemes. Some pairs of children from Group 2 could use the computer to compose their poems.

3*(first): Give each child a copy of the poem and ask them to re-read the poem with expression. Encourage them to make use of the punctuation to guide the way in which they read different lines – they should look especially at question marks and exclamation marks. They should then prepare to read to an audience.

### Conclusion

Ask each group to tell the rest of the class about what they have been doing. Discuss the rhyming words which Group 2 have found and ask Group 3 to read the poem aloud, encouraging the others to follow it carefully and listen to see if the group makes use of the punctuation. Display the word banks and invite the children to make additions.

**Note:** This lesson could be developed into a series focused upon 'The Rescue'. The poem could be used as a starting point for story writing using a similar setting and further work could be done on rhyme.

# THE RESCUE

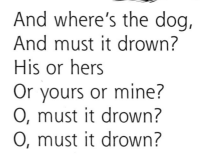

The wind is loud,
The wind is blowing,
The waves are big,
The waves are growing.
What's that? What's that?
A dog is crying,
It's in the sea,
A dog is crying,
His or hers
Or yours or mine?
A dog is crying,
A dog is crying.

Is no one there?
A boat is going,
The waves are big,
A man is rowing,
The waves are big,
The waves are growing.
Where's the dog?
It isn't crying.
His or hers
Or yours or mine?
Is it dying?
Is it dying?

The wind is loud,
The wind is blowing,
The waves are big,
The waves are growing.
Where's the boat?
It's upside down.

And where's the dog,
And must it drown?
His or hers
Or yours or mine?
O, must it drown?
O, must it drown?

Where's the man?
He's on the sand,
So tired and wet
He cannot stand.
And where's the dog?
It's in his hand,
He lays it down
Upon the sand.
His or hers
Or yours or mine?
The dog is mine,
The dog is mine!

So tired and wet
And still it lies.
I stroke its head,
It opens its eyes,
It wags its tail,
So tired and wet.
I call its name,
For it's my pet,
Not his or hers
Or yours, but mine –
And up it gets,
And up it gets!

*Ian Serraillier*

# LITTLE RED RIDING HOOD

## OBJECTIVES

| UNIT | SPELLING AND VOCABULARY | GRAMMAR AND PUNCTUATION | COMPREHENSION AND COMPOSITION |
|------|-------------------------|-------------------------|-------------------------------|
| READING AND WRITING FICTION 'Little Red Riding Hood' and other traditional stories. | Learn new words linked to a story. Revise the use of the grapheme oo (short as in good and long as in moon). | Secure the use of simple sentences in own writing. Use commas to separate items in a list. Use speech marks in dialogue. | Identify and describe characters in a story. Write a story in the same setting as 'Little Red Riding Hood'. Discuss story settings and talk about their influence upon events and behaviour. |

## ORGANIZATION (5 HOURS)

| | INTRODUCTION | WHOLE-CLASS SKILLS WORK | DIFFERENTIATED GROUP ACTIVITIES | CONCLUSION |
|--|--------------|------------------------|--------------------------------|------------|
| HOUR 1 | Shared reading of 'Little Red Riding Hood'. Discussion about its sequence of events. | Revise spelling of words that include the grapheme oo. | 1*(second): Guided reading and discussion. Prepare to read to an audience. 2*(first): Write a sequence of events. 3: Refer to notes and prepare to re-tell the story. | Discussion about the events of the story. Group 3 to re-tell the story. |
| HOUR 2 | Discussion of characters in 'Little Red Riding Hood'. Make character profiles. | Look at ways of presenting text. | 1: Write a sequence of events. 2: Produce character profiles using diagrams. 3*:Guided reading with expression. | Look at character profiles produced by Group 2 and create a word bank of adjectives. Focus upon words containing the grapheme oo and look at spellings. |
| HOUR 3 | Reading of excerpt from story and discussion about characters. | Write sentences including commas in lists of adjectives. | 1*: Refer to notes and prepare to re-tell story. 2: Guided reading with expression. 3: Write character profiles using commas for lists. | Look at Group 3's sentences about characters and at commas in lists. |
| HOUR 4 | Look at character profiles and descriptions of characters from other stories. | Introduce the class story and introduce secretarial features. | 1: Write a character profile using phrases and sentences. 2: Write a character profile using appropriate adjectives and justifying their description. 3*: Re-read with expression. Prepare to read to an audience. | Discussion about story plot and characters. |
| HOUR 5 | Shared discussion about characters. Match samples of speech to characters. | Look at speech marks and unfamiliar words. | 1: Read other versions of the story with expression. 2*: Write a character profile using sentences and examples of speech. 3: Match spoken text to each character. | Discussion about characters and dialogue. Compare versions of the story. |

## RESOURCES

Photocopiable pages 115 and 116 ('Little Red Riding Hood'), copies of any other version of the Little Red Riding Hood story, a set of cards on which have been written the four characters in the story, a set of cards of adjectives describing the characters and some blank cards, a book of any other traditional stories with which the children may be familiar, board or flip chart, plenty of paper, writing materials.

## PREPARATION

Prepare sufficient copies of photocopiable pages 115 and 116 for each child to have one and prepare an enlarged version or OHT of the same pages. Prepare a set of cards with the names of the four characters from the story written on and a set with a variety of adjectives describing them. You should also have blank cards for you to write the children's suggestions on. Have ready a book of other traditional stories (or make a copy of one story) to read to the class. Prepare a Big Book version of the story (see 'Big Books', page 10 of the Introduction).

### Introduction and whole-class skills work

**Note:** 'Little Red Riding Hood' is a traditional tale with a variety of possible endings. The version on the photocopiable page here is less bloodthirsty than most. Children may know other versions. The tale also involves a child setting off alone into woods. This may provide an opportunity to remind the children of the danger of leaving friends when playing and of talking to strangers.

Begin by asking the children to suggest some well-known stories and to tell you where they are set. Read any well-known traditional story to the children and ask them to tell you about it. Ask them where the story was set and discuss the place and time.

Ask the children to help you to tell the story of 'Little Red Riding Hood'. As they tell you each section of the story, make brief notes on the board or flip chart of the key words. Discuss with the children which words you will need to write down to help them to remember the story.

There may be some dispute about the events in the story. If this is the case, note the alternatives which the children suggest. Discuss, in particular, the settings in which the story takes place – Red Riding Hood's house, the woods, Grandma's house. List these on the board and ask the children to suggest descriptions. You might ask them why the woods might be scary and why Red Riding Hood's own house might be a safe place. You could also list the events which take place in each setting.

Look with the children at some of the words which you have written and discuss their spellings. The children should already be familiar with the 'oo' sound in 'good', so this may be an opportunity to look at 'hood' and 'wood'. They should also know the 'oo' sound in 'moon' from their work in Year 1, so this is an opportunity to use both and show the distinction. Words which may arise during the telling of the story include:

| | | | | |
|---|---|---|---|---|
| *good* | *hood* | *wood* | *food* | *look* |
| *took* | *book* | *crooked* | *soon* | |

### Differentiated group activities

1*(second): Provide this group with copies of photocopiable pages 115 and 116 ('Little Red Riding Hood') and ask them to practise reading it with expression. They should then prepare to read to an audience.

2*(first): Ask the children to list the sequence of events in the story using single words or short phrases. Encourage them to use numbers or arrows to make the order clear. Some pairs of children from Group 2 could use the computer for this activity.

3: Ask the children to refer to the notes which you made with the class and to add their own notes concerning the events, settings and characters of the story. They should then prepare to tell the story to the rest of the class from their notes.

### Conclusion

Ask each group to tell the rest of the class about the work they have done. Children from Group 2 should relate the sequence of events and those in Group 3 should use their notes to tell the story.

### Introduction and whole-class skills work

Begin the lesson by discussing the story of Little Red Riding Hood and then explain that Group 1 have been practising reading it and will be reading it aloud. If necessary, read with the children and re-read the story yourself when they have finished to provide a good model.

Ask the children to tell you about the characters and then write the names Little Red Riding Hood, Wolf, Grandma and Father on the board, leaving sufficient space for you to write appropriate adjectives around them. Invite the children to suggest adjectives which would describe each.

Explain that it is not always necessary to write sentences to provide information and that it is possible to provide it using diagrams and charts. Use the examples produced by Group 2 in the previous lesson to illustrate this.

### Differentiated group activities

1: Read and sequence text activity (as Group 2, Hour 1).
2: Ask the children to continue to produce character profiles using diagrams. This should follow up the work done during the previous lesson and reinforce the use of different presentational devices.
3*: Guided reading with expression (as Group 1, Hour 1).

### Conclusion

Look at the character profiles produced by Group 2 and build up a word bank of adjectives which could be used to describe people and wolves (see 'How to make a word bank', page 10 of the Introduction). Focus upon the spellings of words which include the grapheme 'oo' and make a list of these.

### Introduction and whole-class skills work

Read an excerpt from the Little Red Riding Hood story and ask the children to think carefully about the characters that are mentioned. When you have finished reading, ask some children to come to the front and hold cards which bear the names of the principal characters. Hold up in turn some of the adjectives which you have written on cards and ask the children to decide which characters could be described by them.

Begin by showing to, and discussing with the children, the notes which Group 2 made about the characters in the story. Write each character's name on the board and then write some of the notes that the group made. Explain again that there are different ways of writing and that making notes can help you to remember things and can provide a starting point for writing in more detail. Ask the children if they have any more ideas about the characters and add these to the lists.

Use another board or flip chart to begin to write sentences about the characters with the children's help. Discuss the use of punctuation and focus upon the use of commas in lists. When the opportunity arises, talk about ways of splitting words up into syllables to help with spelling. Mention, too, the need for capital letters for names and for the beginnings of sentences.

### Differentiated group activities

1*: Prepare to re-tell the story from notes (as Group 3, Hour 1).
2: Re-read the story. Prepare to read to an audience.
3: Ask the children to write character profiles in complete sentences using commas to separate list of adjectives. You may need to provide the children with starting points such as The wolf is... and access to the word bank of adjectives.

### Conclusion

Ask Group 3 to show their sentences and write some of these on the board. Discuss the adjectives which have been used and ask the children to help you to put commas in the correct places in lists.

### Introduction and whole-class skills work

Children will be working towards the production of a class Big Book version of the story. This could be done as part of further literacy hours or at another time set aside for extended writing.

Explain to the children that they are going to make a class story book. Talk with them about the ways in which authors work and discuss the notes which have been made and the sentences which were written in the previous lesson. The audience for the story could be younger children within the school.

Discuss with the class the character profiles which the groups have made and explain that Group 1 will be using these and their own ideas to write in more detail in sentences about the characters. Read some extracts from other stories in which there is a description of a character and talk with the children about the authors' use of language.

Talk with the children about the features of a book and discuss the jobs which will need to be done if the book is to be successful. This should provide an opportunity to discuss the need for punctuation and capital letters and for accurate spelling. Add to the word bank any words which the children think they may need when writing.

### Differentiated group activities

1: Ask the children to write a profile of one of the characters from the story in complete sentences, drawing upon their own ideas and those produced by Group 2 in Hour 2 and Group 3 in Hour 3.

2: Ask the children to write character profiles of Little Red Riding Hood and the wolf. Discuss the adjectives which they might use to describe each character and list these under the character's name. Then ask the children to justify their descriptions and encourage them to write sentences which include the adjectives. For example, they might describe Red Riding Hood as 'kind' and then write: 'I think Red Riding Hood was kind because she took a basket of food to her grandmother.' Some pairs of children from Group 2 could use the computer for this activity.

3*: Guided reading with expression (as Group 1, Hour 1).

### Conclusion

Ask each group to tell the rest of the class about the work they have been doing. Talk through the story plot with them and discuss the characters.

### Introduction and whole-class skills work

Discuss the story with the children and read to them some of the words which were spoken by different characters and ask them to suggest who might have spoken. Repeat this exercise, using another traditional tale which all of the children are likely to know.

Show the children on the board or OHT some samples of speech including speech marks, the verb and any other words which denote the speaker but leave a space with a line where the speaker's name would be. Discuss the speech marks and their job and ask the children to think carefully about who might have said the words. If they find this difficult, offer them a choice of characters. Ask them to justify the one they choose and encourage them to talk about the characters and express their views about them. Look at any words which are unfamiliar to the children and write these on the board and help them to spell them.

### Differentiated group activities

1: Ask the children to read copies of any other versions of the story with expression and to prepare to read them to an audience.

2*: Work with the children to produce character profiles using phrases and sentences and examples of speech. You might draw a simple picture of each character in the centre of a piece of paper and then use the children's suggestions to write examples of things which the character said and did which indicate the sort of person he or she is. Pairs of children from Group 2 could use the computer for this activity (possibly with a program which enables them to place text around a central picture).

3: Provide a selection of pieces of spoken text and ask the children to match each to a character from the story. Encourage them to refer to the text to enable them to match the quotations.

### Conclusion

Ask Group 3 to read out some of their quotations and ask the others to identify them. Remind the children about using adjectives to describe characters. Ask the children in Group 1 to read aloud some extracts from the version of the story which they have read and discuss the ways in which it differs from the photocopiable version.

# LITTLE RED RIDING HOOD

One day a little girl set out from her house to visit her grandmother. The little girl always wore her favourite coat which was bright red with a red hood. Everyone called her Little Red Riding Hood because of the coat she wore.

Little Red Riding Hood's grandmother lived in a little house in the woods and the little girl had to walk through the trees on a narrow path to get there. She carried a basket full of food which her mother had prepared for her grandmother. There was tea, sugar, bread, butter, an apple pie, and a special cake with cherries in it.

Before she left home, Little Red Riding Hood's father, who was a woodcutter, told her not to talk to strangers and especially to beware of the wicked wolf who lived in the woods.

As she was walking through the woods, Little Red Riding Hood did not see the wicked wolf hiding behind trees and watching her skipping and running to her grandmother's house. He ran through the woods as quickly as he could and climbed through a window into Grandmother's house. Before Grandmother could do or say anything, he tied her up and put her into a cupboard and locked the door. Then he quickly dressed himself in Grandmother's frilly nightcap, climbed into bed and pulled the sheets right up to his chin.

When Little Red Riding Hood reached her grandmother's house she gave her special knock on the door and she heard a voice call, "Come in my dear."

She went into the house and called, "Grandma where are you?"

"I'm in here my dear," called the wolf from the bedroom. "Come and see me. Have you brought me some nice things?"

Little Red Riding Hood opened the bedroom door and looked at the wolf. "Oh Grandma," she said, "What big eyes you've got!"

"All the better to see you with, my dear!" replied the wolf.

Then she saw two big ears sticking out below the nightcap. "Oh Grandma," she said, "What big ears you've got!"

# LITTLE RED RIDING HOOD (CONTINUED)

"All the better to hear you with, my dear!" replied the wolf.

Then she saw two big paws holding the sheet. "Oh Grandma," she said, "What big hands you've got!"

"All the better to hug you with, my dear!" replied the wolf.

Little Red Riding Hood thought that something was wrong. She looked at the wolf's smiling face and said, "Oh Grandma," she said, "What big teeth you've got!"

"All the better to eat you with, my dear!" replied the wolf and as he said it, he jumped from the bed and leaped across the room towards her. The wolf chased her round and round the house. Little Red Riding Hood was so frightened that she screamed. She screamed so loudly that her father, who was cutting wood nearby, heard her and rushed to the house. As soon as he saw the wolf he raised his axe and shouted to the wolf to get out of the house. The wolf ran away so fast and so far that he never came back to the woods again.

Father chased him for a little while, then he came back to the house to make sure that his daughter was safe. They both heard banging coming from the inside of the cupboard which the wolf had locked. Father broke down the door with his axe and they found Grandmother safe and sound inside. So they untied her and made her a cup of tea.

As she sat at the kitchen table drinking her tea, Grandma smiled and said, "It's nice to have a bit of excitement for a change!"

Little Red Riding Hood and her father looked at each other and they smiled too. Father made them all something to eat. They had bread and butter and strawberry jam and a slice of delicious cake with cherries in it.

# GETTING READY FOR SCHOOL

## OBJECTIVES

| UNIT | SPELLING AND VOCABULARY | GRAMMAR AND PUNCTUATION | COMPREHENSION AND COMPOSITION |
|------|-------------------------|-------------------------|-------------------------------|
| READING FICTION 'Getting ready for school'. | Learn new words related to a particular topic. | Use a variety of ways of presenting texts. | Use flow charts to explain a process. |

## ORGANIZATION (2 HOURS)

| | INTRODUCTION | WHOLE-CLASS SKILLS WORK | DIFFERENTIATED GROUP ACTIVITIES | CONCLUSION |
|---|--------------|------------------------|--------------------------------|------------|
| HOUR 1 | Shared reading of 'Getting ready for school'. | Raise phonological awareness by looking at new words. | 1: Prepare flow charts to show to the rest of the class. 2: Read and sequence text. 3*: Guided reading and listing of key events. | Select pupils from each of the groups to read and present their work. Discuss responses. Display flow charts. |
| HOUR 2 | Shared re-reading of 'Getting ready for school'. Discussion of another simple process. | Look at different ways of presenting text. | 1*: Guided reading and putting key events into a flow chart. 2: Prepare flow charts to show to the rest of the class. 3: Read and sequence text. | Group 1 show flow chart made with teacher to the rest of the class. Group 2 show flow chart of 'Getting ready for school'. |

## RESOURCES

Photocopiable page 119 ('Getting ready for school'), samples of flow charts showing approximately six stages (for example, brushing teeth), a copy of a piece of writing which has clear progression which could be identified in a flow chart (you might use a poem such as 'There Was an Old Woman Who Swallowed a Fly'), board or flip chart, writing materials.

## PREPARATION

Make enough copies of photocopiable page 119 ('Getting ready for school') for each child to have a copy. Make two sets of the sentences on photocopiable page 119 written on individual cards. Write on the board or flip chart or prepare an OHT of a flow chart of an activity which will be familiar to the children.

### Introduction and whole-class skills work

Show the children either an enlarged version or an OHT of a flow chart for a familiar activity such as brushing teeth. The chart should include about six stages and words should be limited and phrases concise – for example, use 'Unscrew cap on toothpaste' rather than 'First you unscrew the cap on the toothpaste'.

Read the chart with the children, then cover it and ask the children to describe the process. Write down some of their more complete sentences on the board or flip chart and then compare these with the simple phrasing on the chart. Explain that sometimes we need to set out information in a simple way rather than in complete sentences and that flow charts and lists enable us to do this.

Ask the children to help you to make a flow chart on the board for another familiar activity. Discuss the way in which words such as 'the', 'you', 'a' and words related to the language of time are unnecessary when information is presented in this way.

Explain that the children are going to be looking at a piece of writing called 'Getting ready for school' and that they will be making their own flow charts. Read 'Getting ready for school' (photocopiable page 119) with the children, and discuss the content. Examine the vocabulary and help the children to learn how to spell some of the more challenging words and any of those which appear in the high frequency List 1. Some of the new vocabulary may include:

uniform     cereal     orange     juice     bowl     comb     goodbye

### Differentiated group activities
1: Give each child a copy of photocopiable page 119 ('Getting ready for school') and ask them to re-read the text and to make a flow chart to show the key events. If they have time, they could go on to make a second flow chart showing the sequence of events they go through themselves when getting ready for school.
2: Give the children a version of photocopiable page 119 ('Getting ready for school') which has been cut up and presented as separate sentences on individual pieces of paper. Ask the children to put the events into the right order and then make a list using key words from each sentence to denote each event. For example, for the sentence 'Next, I go to my bedroom and get dressed in my school uniform', they might write 'Get dressed'. Some pairs of children from Group 2 could use the computer for this activity.
3*: Give the children a copy of photocopiable page 119 and re-read it to them. Produce a flow chart on the board of the events described and discuss the vocabulary.

### Conclusion
Ask each group to tell the rest of the class about the flow charts and lists which they produced. Group 1 should show their charts and explain to the class what each section represents. Display the flow charts.

### Introduction and whole-class skills work
Begin by looking with the children at 'Getting ready for school' again and talk with them about the flow charts which some produced. Now introduce another process such as 'Writing a story' and ask the children to help you to write six sentences which describe the process. As you write on the board or flip chart, encourage children to discuss punctuation and spelling and discuss any unfamiliar words.

When you have six sentences, ask the children if they can help you to make a flow chart to show the events in a different form. Discuss once again the key words in each sentence and talk about the way in which the chart can be set out. You may wish to draw arrows on lines connecting each event to show the children the order in which things happen.

### Differentiated group activities
1*: Guided reading exercise (as Group 3, Hour 1).
2: Preparing flow charts exercise (as Group 1, Hour 1).
3: Read and sequence text activity (as Group 2, Hour 1).
Children in all groups who finish their work early could go on to produce further flow charts for other processes.

### Conclusion
Show the class some of the flow charts which the children have made and discuss the way in which these have been organized. Talk about other ways of organizing text without writing complete sentences and discuss the spelling of some of the key words.

# GETTING READY FOR SCHOOL

I get out of bed at eight o'clock and go to the bathroom to have a wash.

Next, I go to my bedroom and get dressed in my school uniform.

After that, I go downstairs and have a bowl of cereal and some orange juice for breakfast.

When I have eaten my breakfast, I go upstairs to the bathroom and I clean my teeth.

When I get downstairs my mum and dad always ask me if I have combed my hair so I go back upstairs and get out the comb.

Finally, I put on my coat, pick up my bag, and say goodbye to my little sister and I set off with my mum or my dad to walk to school.

# SWIMMING AFTER SCHOOL

## OBJECTIVES

| UNIT | SPELLING AND VOCABULARY | GRAMMAR AND PUNCTUATION | COMPREHENSION AND COMPOSITION |
|---|---|---|---|
| READING AND WRITING FICTION 'Swimming after school'. | Spell words with common prefixes to indicate the negative. Explore the use of antonyms. | Use awareness of grammar to decipher new words. Explore the need for grammatical agreement in writing. | Use phonological, contextual, grammatical and graphic knowledge to work out, predict and check the meanings of unfamiliar words. Use shared and guided writing to apply phonological and graphic knowledge and sight vocabulary to spell words accurately. Reinforce and apply word level skills through shared reading. |

## ORGANIZATION (4 HOURS)

| | INTRODUCTION | WHOLE-CLASS SKILLS WORK | DIFFERENTIATED GROUP ACTIVITIES | CONCLUSION |
|---|---|---|---|---|
| HOUR 1 | Shared reading of 'Swimming after school'. | Discussion about antonyms. Development of a word bank. | 1: Read with expression. Prepare to read to an audience. 2*: Read text and identify words with the prefixes un- and dis-. Identify words with antonyms. 3: Explore un- and dis- words using a dictionary. | Look at words with antonyms. Develop a word bank. |
| HOUR 2 | Shared re-reading of 'Swimming after school' in its original and opposite version. | Match antonyms from the two texts. Discuss antonyms. | 1*: Guided reading of 'Swimming after school'. Discussion about antonyms. 2: Write a continuation of the story 'Swimming after school'. 3: Make a word bank of antonyms. | Discussion about antonyms that could be used to change the meaning of 'Swimming after school'. |
| HOUR 3 | Shared writing of a simple story that includes words that have antonyms. | Look at spellings of common antonyms. | 1: Write a continuation of the story 'Swimming after school'. 2: Make a word bank of antonyms. 3*: Guided reading of 'Swimming after school'. Discussion about antonyms. | Look at the antonyms that feature in Group 1's activities. |
| HOUR 4 | Look at sentences that include antonyms. | Continued look at antonyms. | 1: Make a word bank of antonyms. 2*: Guided reading of 'Swimming after school'. Discussion about antonyms. 3: Play the antonym game. | Look at the antonym cards and play the game as a class. |

### RESOURCES

Photocopiable pages 124 ('Swimming after school – 1'), 125 ('Swimming after school – 2') and 126 ('Opposites'), a copy of the text about Paul (below), dictionaries, board or flip chart, writing materials.

### PREPARATION

Make enough copies of photocopiable pages 124 and 125 for each child to have one. Make a set of 'antonym cards' by cutting up the words on photocopiable page 126 or writing them on separate pieces of card. Make enlarged copies of pages 124 and 125 or make OHTs of each text.

**HOUR 1**

### Introduction and whole-class skills work

Read this piece of text to the children and ask them to tell you about it.

> *Paul was very happy. It was his birthday. His father had made tea. There were lots of things to eat that he really liked. He would be able to eat a lot of healthy foods.*

Write the prefixes 'dis-' and 'un-' on the board or flip chart and ask the children if they can use them to change the meaning of the passage. Talk to them about opposites and explain that some words relate to other words that have different meanings while others can be changed by putting a prefix in front of them. You will need to point out to the children that not all words that begin with 'un-' or 'dis-' are negatives. For example, they should not confuse words such as 'united' and 'union' with negatives since the 'uni-' beginning means 'one'.

Ask the children to help you to change the text by using prefixes. Discuss with them other words that begin with 'dis-' or 'un-' where the prefixes indicate the negative. Start a class word bank and add any new words to it.

### Differentiated group activities

1: Ask the children to re-read photocopiable page 124 ('Swimming after school – 1') with expression. Encourage the children to take turns to read and to think of an ending for the story that they could tell in their own words. They should then prepare to read to an audience.

2*: Give the children copies of photocopiable page 125 and ask them to re-read the text. Ask them to identify words with the prefixes 'un-' or 'dis-' and words with antonyms.

3: Provide the children with dictionaries and ask them to find words that begin with 'un-' or 'dis-' and to make a list of them.

### Conclusion

Ask Group 1 to tell the rest of the class how they would end 'Swimming after school – 1' and to read the story aloud. Discuss words with antonyms and add these to the class word bank.

### Introduction and whole-class skills work

**Note:** Photocopiable page 125 ('Swimming after school –2') is an amended version of photocopiable page 124 with antonyms substituted for many words. The children may look at the text and suggest that other words could be changed. For example, they might argue that verbs such as 'walking' could be changed to 'running'. They should be encouraged to look at the text in this way, but it may be easier for most children if you focus upon nouns, adjectives and adverbs and leave verbs as they are. They may, however, insert words such as 'not' next to verbs to provide an opposite meaning if you think this is appropriate.

Begin by talking about the story 'Swimming after school' that the children read in the previous lesson and ask them to read it again with you. Talk about the way in which the story could be changed if some of the words were changed to their antonyms.

Show the children the first part of the story that has been changed and ask the children to compare it with the original. Ideally, you should show the two pieces at the same time. Ask the children to tell you which words have been changed and invite them to explain what this does to the meaning of the text. Write on the board or flip chart each word that has been changed next to the one that has been substituted and begin to build up a word bank of antonyms. Explain that not every word has been changed and that they could look for others that could be changed. Talk with the children about the spelling patterns in the words and help them to learn how to spell some of the words.

### Differentiated group activities

1*: Re-read 'Swimming after school – 1' with the children. Ask them to make a note of any words that they think have opposites and to list the words in pairs.

2: Ask the children to write an ending for the story. Some pairs of children from Group 2 could use the computer for this activity.

3: Ask the children to make a dictionary of antonyms. Encourage them to use some of the words that have been put into the word bank and then to write a definition or a sentence that includes the words.

### Conclusion

Ask each group to tell the rest of the class about the work that they have been doing. Discuss how the meaning of the text can be changed through the use of antonyms.

### Introduction and whole-class skills work

Tell the children that you want them to help you to write the beginning of a short story on the board. Discuss possible themes and explain that you would like to include as many words that have antonyms as possible. Use the list that you made in the previous lesson or draw upon the children's ideas.

As you write the story, discuss what you are doing with the children. Use their words, but when they suggest phrasing that is grammatically incorrect (for example, 'we was') use this as a starting point for discussion. Encourage the children to consider the positioning of commas and full stops and the use of capital letters and let them see that you form letters correctly.

When the story is complete ask the children to read it through with you and look for words that could be replaced by their antonyms. Write some of these above the original words and ask the children to read the new versions with you. Talk about the changes to meaning that the antonyms make and ask the children to think about which versions they prefer.

### Differentiated group activities

1: Ask the children to continue the story that the whole class was writing. Encourage them to make use of the list of antonyms that may be provided as a word bank.
2: Making a dictionary and forming sentences using antonyms (as Group 3, Hour 2). Some pairs of children from Group 2 could use the computer for this activity.
3*: Guided reading activity (as Group 1, Hour 2).

### Conclusion

Ask Group 1 to read their continuations of the class story and make a note on the board of any antonyms that they use. Discuss the words and their spellings with the class.

### Introduction and whole-class skills work

Begin by discussing the story 'Swimming after school' –1 and reminding the children about antonyms. Next, write some sentences on the board and ask the children to read them with you and to suggest antonyms that could be used to change meaning. Each time an antonym is suggested, write it on the board and discuss whether it would fit into the sentence and the way in which it should be spelled.

### Differentiated group activities

1: Making a dictionary and forming sentences using antonyms (as Group 3, Hour 2). Some pairs of children from Group 1 could use the computer for this activity.
2*: Guided reading activity (as Group 1, Hour 2).
3: Ask the children to arrange the cards (made from photocopiable page 126) so that pairs of words are made. Some words have more than one antonym. Encourage the children to look out for these.

### Conclusion

Give each child one of the antonym cards. On further cards add any words that have been discovered during the series of lessons. Ask the children in turn to come out to the front and hold up and read their cards. Then invite other children to say if they have words that are antonyms of the words held up. Write down the pairs of words and discuss their spellings as you do so.

# SWIMMING AFTER SCHOOL – 1

It was a hot, sunny day. Sam was walking home from school with his father. The roads were dry and when he stopped to tie his shoelace, Sam could feel that the pavement was hot to touch.

Sam and his father were feeling happy. The swimming pool was open and they were going to go for a swim before tea.

"You will have to have a wash before we go into the pool, Sam," said his father. "The pool will turn black if you get in to it covered with all that dirt."

Sam looked at his hands and knees. They were dirty from playing football on the school field. His team had won and Sam had been the goalkeeper. He had stopped lots of shots and had covered himself in soil.

Sam didn't mind having a wash. It was kind of his father to take him to the pool and he did not want to make him cross by grumbling about having to wash. He really liked swimming and he ran upstairs to the bathroom as soon as he got home.

"Don't leave the bathroom untidy!" his father shouted from the bottom of the stairs.

"I won't, Dad!" Sam called back.

After he had washed, Sam went into his bedroom and found his trunks and towel and then went quickly downstairs. His father was waiting for him at the front door. "Right, let's go!" he said, and the two of them set off down the road to the pool.

It was very noisy at the pool. Children were jumping into the water and sliding down the water chute. Sam saw his best friend, Jo, being pushed under the water by Sarah Smith. Before his father had time to stop him, Sam jumped into the pool and swam to help Jo. He was going to have a really good time.

# SWIMMING AFTER SCHOOL – 2

It was a cold, cloudy night. Sam was walking home to school without her mother. The roads were wet and when she started to untie her shoelace, Sam could feel that the pavement was cold to touch.

Sam and her mother were feeling unhappy. The swimming pool was closed and they were not going to go for a swim after tea.

"You will not have to have a wash after we go out of the pool, Sam," said her mother. "The pool will turn white if you get out of it uncovered without all that dirt."

Sam did not look at her hands and knees. They were clean from playing football on the school field. Her team had lost and Sam had been the goalkeeper. She had stopped lots of shots and had uncovered herself in soil.

Sam did mind having a wash. It was unkind of her mother to take her to the pool and she did not want to make her cross by grumbling about having to wash. She really disliked swimming and she ran downstairs to the bathroom as soon as she got home.

"Do leave the bathroom tidy!" her mother shouted from the top of the stairs.

"I will, Mum!" Sam called back.

Before she had washed, Sam went out of her bedroom and lost her trunks and towel and then went slowly upstairs. Her mother was waiting for her at the back door. "Right, let's stay!" she said, and the two of them set off up the road to the pool.

It was very quiet at the pool. Children were jumping out of the water and sliding up the water chute. Sam saw her worst friend, Jo, being pushed over the water by Sarah Smith. After her mother had time to stop her, Sam jumped out of the pool and swam to help Jo. She was going to have a really bad time.

# OPPOSITES

| | | | | |
|---|---|---|---|---|
| hot | wet | high | cold | big |
| full | small | tall | dry | empty |
| hard | low | true | soft | happy |
| sad | like | bad | under | good |
| unlike | easy | tie | on | untie |
| unhappy | untrue | thick | up | thin |
| down | short | obey | far | disobey |
| long | near | off | over | dislike |

# WHAT IS RED?

## OBJECTIVES

| UNIT | SPELLING AND VOCABULARY | GRAMMAR AND PUNCTUATION | COMPREHENSION AND COMPOSITION |
|------|------------------------|------------------------|------------------------------|
| READING AND WRITING POETRY 'What is Red? | Segment words into phonemes for spelling. | Re-read own writing to check that it makes sense. | Use simple poem structures to write poems collectively and individually. |

## ORGANIZATION (3 HOURS)

| | INTRODUCTION | WHOLE-CLASS SKILLS WORK | DIFFERENTIATED GROUP ACTIVITIES | CONCLUSION |
|---|---|---|---|---|
| HOUR 1 | Shared reading of 'What is Red? by Mary O'Neill. Shared writing of a poem. | Raise awareness of rhymes. Make a collection of rhyming words. | 1: Explore rhyming words and write poems. 2: Re-read with expression. Prepare to read to an audience. 3*: Develop a class poem and substitute own ideas. | Select pupils from Group 1 to read and present their work. Discuss responses. Display new rhymes. Group 2 to read the poem to the class. |
| HOUR 2 | Shared re-reading of 'What is Red? | Segment words into phonemes to help children with spelling. | 1: Re-read with expression. Prepare to read to an audience. 2*: Develop a class poem and substitute own ideas. 3: Explore rhyming words and write poems. | Select pupils from Group 3 to read and present their work. Discuss responses. Display new rhymes. Group 1 to read the poem to the class. |
| HOUR 3 | Shared reading of nursery rhymes and other traditional verses. | Raise phonological awareness by assonance. | 1*: Write a group colour poem. 2: Explore rhyming words and write poems. 3: Re-read with expression, Prepare to read to an audience. | Select pupils from Groups 1 and 2 to read and present |

## RESOURCES

Photocopiable page 130 ('What is Red?' by Mary O'Neill), a book of other traditional verse such as nursery rhymes, board or flip chart, paper, writing materials. For their Hour 2 activity, Group 3 may need a word bank (see 'How to make a word bank', page 10 of the Introduction).

## PREPARATION

Prepare an enlarged version or OHT of the poem 'What is Red?' and sufficient copies for each child to have one.

### Introduction and whole-class skills work

Ask the children what they think of when they think of the colour red. Write the word 'red' in the middle of the board and write the children's suggestions around it.

Read the poem 'What is Red?' to the children and discuss the ideas which the poet has about the colour red. Now tell the children that you are going to write a poem together using their ideas and any new ones which the poem has given them. Ask the children to tell you what to write and record it on the board. Do not be afraid to change lines if the children suggest amendments. The poem should be no more than eight lines long. This should make them aware of the processes which poets go through before presenting a finished poem.

Concentrate at first upon writing down ideas, but later ask the children if they think the poem should rhyme. It may be possible to rearrange sentences and to change the order of the lines to make it rhyme.

Encourage the children to think about possible rhymes and write some of their ideas for pairs of rhyming words next to the poem. Tell the children that you intend to complete the poem with them later.

### Differentiated group activities

1: Ask the children to write their own short poems about the colour red. You may wish to provide them with a structure for doing this, depending upon the ability of the children. One possibility would be to ask them to write a rhyming second line for the line: 'I really love the colour red'. The line could be repeated four times so that children might write something like:

> I really love the colour red.
> It makes me think of jam on bread.
> I really love the colour red.
> It makes me think of roses in a flower bed.
> I really love the colour red.
>     and so on...

Alternatively, they might substitute words such as 'hate', 'fear' and 'like' for 'love' in all the lines or some of them. Some pairs of children from Group 1 could use the computer for this activity.

2: Provide the children with copies of the poem and ask them to re-read and learn it. They should then prepare to recite it in front of the rest of the class.

3*: Ask the children to look at the poem which you have been writing on the board and invite them to rewrite it and make it rhyme.

### Conclusion

Ask Group 1 to read the poems they have written to the rest of the class. Now ask the class to help you to improve the poem you were writing earlier, making particular use of the ideas suggested by Group 1. Ask Group 2 to read this poem to the class. Display the rhymes.

### Introduction and whole-class skills work

Begin by re-reading 'What is Red?' and then suggest to the children that they could help you to write a poem about a different colour. When a colour has been decided upon, ask the children to help you to prepare to write it by suggesting lots of words which rhyme with the colour (blue, green and white are suitable as they have several rhymes).

Make a point of drafting, editing and revising the poem as you write it on the board or flip chart and invite the children to read it and suggest changes as you go along. Discuss spellings and show the children how they can segment words and identify the part which forms the rhyme or rime. Talk about layout. Make sure that the children see and discuss correct letter formation.

### Differentiated group activities

1: Re-read with expression. Prepare to read to an audience (as Group 2, Hour 1).
2*: Development of class poem (as Group 3, Hour 1).
3: Explore rhyming words and write own poems (as Group 1, Hour 1). If necessary, provide Group 3 with a word bank to help them.

### Conclusion

Ask some children from Group 3 to read their poems aloud and invite children to offer help where these are incomplete. Discuss the rhymes which children have found and help them to spell the words. Display the rhymes for the children to see. Ask Group 1 to read the poem to the class.

## HOUR 3

### Introduction and whole-class skills work

Use the beginning of the lesson to read some of the poems which the children have written and to read aloud and show the children traditional verse such as a nursery rhymes. If you use nursery rhymes you will find that some of the rhymes are assonant in that the vowel sound is repeated but the final consonant sounds of the rhyming couplet differ. For example, in 'Baa Baa Black Sheep' 'dame' and 'lane' are used as rhymes. This could be discussed with the children. Read the nursery rhymes aloud with the children and ask them to emphasize the rhyming words. Write the rhyming words on the board and ask the children if they can think of other words which would rhyme with them.

### Differentiated group activities

1*: Ask the children to look at the poem written as a class during Hour 1. Ask them to write their own poem with a colour theme.

2: Explore rhyming words and write own poems (as Group 1, Hour 1).

3: Re-read with expression. Prepare to read to an audience (as Group 2, Hour 1).

### Conclusion

Ask Groups 1 and 2 to read their poems aloud to the rest of the class. Ask the children to tell you some of the rhyming words which they have found during the unit of lessons and write these on the board or flip chart. Discuss the onset and the rime in the words and discuss assonance again. Display the new rhymes. Finally, ask Group 3 to read the poem to the class.

# WHAT IS RED?

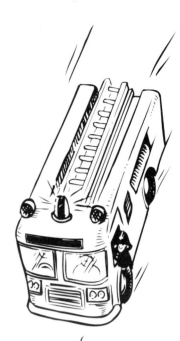

Red is a sunset
Blazing and bright.
Red is feeling brave
With all your might.
Red is a sunburn
Spot on your nose.
Sometimes red
Is a red red rose.
Red squiggles out
When you cut your hand.
Red is a brick
And the sound of a band.
Red is hotness
You get inside.
When you're embarrassed
And want to hide.
Fire-cracker, fire-engine
Fire-flicker red —
And when you're angry
Red runs through your head.
Red is an Indian,
A Valentine heart,
The trimmings on
A circus cart.
Red is a lipstick
Red is a shout
Red is a signal
That says: 'Watch out!'
Red is a great big
Rubber ball.
Red is the giant-est
Colour of all.
Red is a show-off,
No doubt about it —
But can you imagine
Living without it?

*Mary O'Neill*

# A FUNNY THING HAPPENED

## OBJECTIVES

| UNIT | SPELLING AND VOCABULARY | GRAMMAR AND PUNCTUATION | COMPREHENSION AND COMPOSITION |
|------|------------------------|------------------------|-------------------------------|
| READING AND WRITING FICTION 'A Funny Thing Happened'. | Read on sight words from the high frequency List 1. | Predict words from preceding words. | Use context as a cue when reading. Predict story endings. Identify and describe characters. Use a story setting and write a different story in the same setting. |

## ORGANIZATION (3 HOURS)

| | INTRODUCTION | WHOLE-CLASS SKILLS WORK | DIFFERENTIATED GROUP ACTIVITIES | CONCLUSION |
|---|-------------|------------------------|--------------------------------|------------|
| HOUR 1 | Shared reading of the story 'A Funny Thing Happened'. | Learn to read and write new words linked to the story. | 1: Guided reading. Prepare to read to an audience. 2*: Read and complete text. 3: Cloze exercise. | Group 1 to read aloud to the class. Examine some alternative words to fill the gaps. Revise spellings of high frequency words. |
| HOUR 2 | Shared re-reading of 'A Funny Thing Happened'. Discussion about story ending. | Revise spelling of high frequency words. Revise spelling of high frequency words and words linked to the story. | 1: Write notes for an ending to the story. 2: Cloze exercise. 3*: Guided reading. Prepare to read to n audience. | Groups 3 to read aloud. Examine sentences completed by Group 2. |
| HOUR 3 | Shared re-reading of 'A Funny Thing Happened'. | Class work on prediction. | 1: Use notes and complete story. 2*(first): Write incomplete sentences for one another to complete. 3*(second): Write text with missing words. | Group 1 to read some story endings to the class. Further work on prediction using grammar based on work of Groups 2 and 3. |

## RESOURCES

Photocopiable pages 134 and 135 ('A Funny Thing Happened – 1 Incomplete Version'), photocopiable pages 136 and 137 ('A Funny Thing Happened – 2 Complete Version'), photocopiable page 138 ('Finish the Sentences'), a piece of simple text, a list of words taken from List 1 of the National Literacy Strategy, board or flip chart, card, Blu-Tack, writing materials.

## PREPARATION

Make sufficient copies of photocopiable pages 134, 135, 136 and 137 for every child in the class to have one. Make an enlarged version or OHT of photocopiable pages 134 and 135. Make enough copies of photocopiable page 138 for each child in Groups 2 and 3 to have one. Make an enlarged version or OHT of a piece of simple text where you have blanked out some words. Cut out small pieces of card for covering up words and stick Blu-Tack on the back. Write out some of the high frequency words from List 1. Have plenty of paper and writing materials for each of the groups.

### Introduction and whole-class skills work

Show the children an enlarged version or OHT of photocopiable pages 135 and 135 ('A Funny Thing Happened – 1 Incomplete Version') covering all but the first paragraph. The first sentence has been left intact so that children may 'get into' the story. Read the story with the children and ask them if they can tell what the missing words might be. The children should be told that the length of the line showing where a word has been missed is the same whatever the length of the missing word. Every eleventh word has been missed out except where its omission would make the text very difficult to follow.

Look at some more of the text and invite the children to suggest what the missing words might be. Emphasize that there may be more than one word which would fit and that the important thing is to enable the story to make sense.

Discuss the story with the children and ask them what they think might happen next. Read some more of the story but leave a pause when you come to a missing word. Encourage them to see that reading beyond the line will help them to make an informed guess as to what the word might be. Read no more than half of the text during this session.

When reading the text with the children, pay particular attention to those words which appear in List 1 if children experience difficulty in reading them. Look also at any words with which children are unfamiliar. These might include:

| | | | | |
|---|---|---|---|---|
| *alone* | *suddenly* | *slot* | *voice* | |
| *trapped* | *pause* | *answer* | *crowd* | *course* |
| *gathered* | *pointing* | *special* | *blushed* | |

Show the children how they can learn to spell the words by looking closely at them, writing them and then checking them. Write the words on the board or flip chart and break them up into graphemes. Cover each word in turn and ask children to come to the front and try to write the word then uncover the word and ask them to check if they spelled it correctly.

### Differentiated group activities

1: Provide each child with a copy of photocopiable pages 134 and 135 ('A Funny Thing Happened – 1 Incomplete Version'). Encourage them to work out what the missing words might be, but tell them to leave a pause if they are not sure. They should then re-read the text with expression and prepare to read to an audience.

2*: Provide each child with a copy of photocopiable pages 134 and 135 ('A Funny Thing Happened – 1 Incomplete Version'). Ask the children to fill in the blanks but encourage discussion and keep emphasizing that there may often be more than one word which will fit. Some pairs of children could use the computer for this activity if the incomplete sentences are saved as a file.

3: Provide each child with a copy of photocopiable page 138 ('Finish the Sentences') and ask them to read and complete the sentences.

### Conclusion

Ask each group to tell the rest of the class about the work they have been doing. Ask the children in Group 1 to read aloud to the rest of the class. Discuss with the children the alternatives which may be possible in some places in the text which Group 2 have been working on. Write some of the high frequency words on the board or flip chart and revise their spellings with the children.

### Introduction and whole-class skills work

Begin by looking once more at an enlarged version or an OHT of some simple text with missing words. Ensure that the first sentence is left intact and cover up every eleventh word. This could be done by placing pieces of card, secured with Blu-Tack, over the words. Work through the text orally with the children and encourage discussion. Reveal the words gradually and discuss the suggestions which the children made and compare them with the words in the text. In order to encourage the use of phonic as well as semantic cues, you may wish to cover all but the initial phoneme in some words.

Next, show the children an enlarged version or OHT of photocopiable pages 134 and 135 ('A Funny Thing Happened –1 Incomplete Version') and work through the second half of the text before asking the groups to work on their tasks. Talk about what might happen next. Throughout the introduction, draw attention to words from the high frequency List 1 whenever children struggle to read them.

### Differentiated group activities

1: Each child should already have a copy of the text of 'A Funny Thing Happened – 1 Incomplete Version'). Ask them to write notes on a possible ending to the story.
2: Cloze exercise (as Group 3, Hour 1).
3*: Guided reading exercise (as Group 1, Hour 1).

### Conclusion

Ask Group 3 to read aloud with your help. Show the whole class the sentences completed by Group 2 and discuss their answers and invite suggestions from the other children as to what the missing words might be.

### Introduction and whole-class skills work

The initial focus of this lesson will be the same text, but this time the children will be looking at photocopiable pages 136 and 137 ('A Funny Thing Happened'– 2 Complete Version'). Discuss the characters in the story and ask the children to suggest characteristics for each.

Discuss with the children the work which they had done in the previous two lessons and ask them to look closely at the story. Ask them to try to remember some of the words which were missed out. Ask them questions: Did their predictions match the ones in the story? Are there better ways of phrasing the story? Can they find words which could be replaced by other words?

### Differentiated group activities

1: Ask the children to refer to their notes made in Hour 2 and to complete the story 'A funny thing happened'. Encourage the children to re-read the story carefully before beginning and to make use of the setting and the characters. Some pairs of children from Group 1 could use the computer for this activity if the text is saved as a file.z
2*(first): Ask the children to write sentences with missing words for you to complete first and discuss the strategies which you use to decide what a missing word might be. Ask them to go on to write sentences for each other to complete.
3*(second): Ask the children to prepare some sentences with missing words while you are working with Group 2 and encourage them to try to catch you out. The children may need access to a word bank and to copies of the high frequency word list to help them with spellings.

### Conclusion

Ask each group to tell the rest of the class about the work which they have been doing. Ask Groups 2 and 3 to read aloud some of their incomplete sentences and invite others to complete them. Ask some children from Group 1 to read aloud their stories and discuss the endings which they have produced.

**Note:** This series of lessons could be extended to include more work on story settings and characters, more work on prediction, more work on high frequency words, and work on new words which appear within the text.

# A FUNNY THING HAPPENED – 1
# INCOMPLETE VERSION

It was a cold, windy day and Sarah pulled up the hood of her coat as she walked along

the road which led to school. Her friend, Jessica Chambers, was ill and Mrs Chambers

had _____ Sarah that Jessica would be staying in bed. For the first _____

since she had started school two years ago, Sarah walked _____ school alone.

Suddenly, she stopped and looked around her. She _____ she heard a voice.

It seemed to come from the _____box. Sarah had always been told never to talk

to _____ and a talking postbox was certainly strange.

"Help, I'm trapped!" _____ a tiny squeaky voice.

Sarah was sure the voice was _____ from inside the post box. There were lots

of children _____ and running to school all around her and there were

_____ mothers and fathers in the street. She knew she should not _____

to strangers, but surely a postbox could not harm _____.

She stood very close to the tall, red postbox _____ put her ear to the slot

where the letters went. _____ enough, she heard

the voice again.

"Please help me. I _____ get out!"

"Who are you?" asked Sarah. "You must be

_____ small if you can get inside a postbox."

"Help, _____ trapped!" called the voice again.

"Yes, I know," said Sarah, "but _____ are you?"

There was a pause and then the voice _____

again, "Please help me. I can't get out!"

Sarah was _____ rather fed up that the voice kept saying the same

# A FUNNY THING HAPPENED – 1
# INCOMPLETE VERSION (CONTINUED)

_____. "Look," she said, "I'm not going to help you until _____ tell me

who you are!"

She waited for the person _____ the postbox to answer, but instead the voice

said, "_____, I'm trapped!"

"Right, that's it, I'm going!" said Sarah angrily. "I'll _____ my teacher that

you're trapped, but I'm not going to _____ here and talk to you if you don't

answer my _____. I think you're very rude!"

Sarah turned to go and _____ she stopped. A crowd of people had gathered

and they _____ seemed to be looking at her. Before she had time _____

say anything, her friend, Jessica, stepped out from the crowd _____ stood in front

of her.

"I thought you were supposed _____ be ill," said Sarah.

"I'm fine," said Jessica smiling. "But _____ don't look very well. Are you all

right. I'm sure _____ just saw you talking to the postbox."

Everyone began _____ laugh. "But there's someone stuck in there," said Sarah

pointing _____ the postbox.

"What day is it, Sarah?" asked Jessica.

"Friday, _____ course!" replied Sarah.

"And what is the date?"

"It's the first of April, of course, but..." Before Sarah

had time to finish, Jessica spoke. "Now what's so special

about April the first?"

Sarah blushed as Jessica walked towards the postbox smiling.

# A FUNNY THING HAPPENED – 2
## COMPLETE VERSION

It was a cold, windy day and Sarah pulled up the hood of her coat as she walked along the road which led to school. Her friend, Jessica Chambers, was ill and Mrs Chambers had told Sarah that Jessica would be staying in bed. For the first time since she had started school two years ago, Sarah walked to school alone.

Suddenly, she stopped and looked around her. She thought she heard a voice. It seemed to come from the postbox. Sarah had always been told never to talk to strangers and a talking postbox was certainly strange.

"Help, I'm trapped!" called a tiny squeaky voice.

Sarah was sure the voice was coming from inside the postbox. There were lots of children walking and running to school all around her and there were many mothers and fathers in the street. She knew she should not talk to strangers, but surely a postbox could not harm her.

She stood very close to the tall, red post box and put her ear to the slot where the letters went. Sure enough, she heard the voice again.

# A FUNNY THING HAPPENED – 2
# COMPLETE VERSION (CONTINUED)

"Please help me. I can't get out!"

"Who are you?" asked Sarah. "You must be very small if you can get inside a post box."

"Help, I'm trapped!" called the voice again.

"Yes, I know," said Sarah, "but who are you?"

There was a pause and then the voice said again, "Please help me. I can't get out!"

Sarah was becoming rather fed up that the voice kept saying the same thing. "Look," she said, "I'm not going to help you until you tell me who you are!"

She waited fro the person inside the postbox to answer, but instead the voice said, "Help, I'm trapped!"

"Right, that's it, I'm going!" said Sarah angrily. "I'll tell my teacher that you're trapped, but I'm not going to stay here and talk to you if you don't answer my questions. I think you're very rude!"

Sarah turned to go and then she stopped. A crowd of people had gathered and they all seemed to be looking at her. Before she had time to say anything, her friend, Jessica, stepped out from the crowd and stood in front of her.

"I thought you were supposed to be ill," said Sarah.

"I'm fine," said Jessica smiling. "But you don't look very well. Are you all right. I'm sure I just saw you talking to the postbox."

Everyone began to laugh. "But there's someone stuck in there," said Sarah pointing to the postbox.

"What day is it, Sarah?" asked Jessica.

"Friday, of course!" replied Sarah.

"And what is the date?"

"It's the first of April, of course, but..." Before Sarah had time to finish, Jessica spoke. "Now what's so special about April the first?"

Sarah blushed as Jessica walked towards the postbox smiling.

# FINISH THE SENTENCES

Sarah walked down the street on a cold, windy _____ .

Sarah's friend, Jessica, was _____ .

Mrs Chambers told Sarah that Jessica was going to stay in _____ .

It was the first time that Sarah had ever walked to school _____ .

Sarah thought she heard a _____ .

The voice seemed to come from the _____ .

The voice said, "Please help me. I can't get _____ !"

Sarah asked who the person in the postbox _____ .

The voice did not answer Sarah's _____ .

Sarah said that she would tell her _____ .

When Sarah looked around she saw a crowd of _____ .

Jessica spoke to _____ .

Jessica was not really _____ .

The date was the first of _____ .

# Term 3

# TONGUE-TWISTERS

## OBJECTIVES

| UNIT | SPELLING AND VOCABULARY | GRAMMAR AND PUNCTUATION | COMPREHENSION AND COMPOSITION |
|---|---|---|---|
| READING FICTION Tongue-twisters and alliteration. | Revise work on homophones. Learn new words linked to writing. | Read text aloud with intonation and expression. | Write alliterative sentences. |

## ORGANIZATION (2 HOURS)

| | INTRODUCTION | WHOLE-CLASS SKILLS WORK | DIFFERENTIATED GROUP ACTIVITIES | CONCLUSION |
|---|---|---|---|---|
| HOUR 1 | Shared reading of names and adjectives. Creation of alliterative phrases and tongue-twisters. | Revise homophones. Create alliterative phrases. | 1*(first): Guided reading. Explore tongue-twisters. 2*(second): Write alliterative sentences using dictionaries. 3: Create alliterative phrases using name and adjective cards. | Group 2 to read their alliterative sentences to the rest of the class. Discuss spellings. |
| HOUR 2 | Shared reading and writing of alliterative sentences. | Examine the correspondence between phonemes and graphemes. | 1*(second): Write alliterative sentences using dictionaries. 2*(first): Guided reading. Explore tongue-twisters. 3: Create further alliterative phrases using name and adjective cards. | Group 3 to read their alliterative sentences to the rest of the class. Discuss spellings and the correspondence between phonemes and graphemes. |

## RESOURCES

Photocopiable page 142 (Adjectives), card for making word cards, any other examples of alliterative sentences, poetry or prose, dictionaries, board or flip chart, writing materials.

## PREPARATION

Use photocopiable page 142 to make a set of adjective cards. Make a set of cards on which have been written the children's names. Make a set of cards of adjectives which could be used to describe the children and which have the same initial sounds as the set of cards of children's names. All of these cards should be capable of being read anywhere in the classroom. For example, adjectives for initial sounds of popular names could include:

*super    lovely    jolly    happy    magnificent    wonderful*

### Introduction and whole-class skills work

Display some of the adjective cards made from photocopiable page 142 on the board and ask a child to come out and hold up his or her name card. Ask the children to choose a suitable alliterative adjective to go with the name. At first, they may choose only those adjectives which have the same initial grapheme and phoneme but, as they become more confident, encourage them to use words which have the same phonemes but different graphemes – for example, Quiet Kate, Clever Chloe, Fantastic Philippa, Shy Sîan. This should provide a good opportunity to discuss words which have the same

sounds but different spellings (homophones).

If the children are used to using a scheme such as Letterland, they may be familiar with such alliterative descriptions and this lesson could include reinforcement work.

### Differentiated group activities

1*(first): Provide the children with copies of examples of tongue-twisters from poetry. Read these with the children. Discuss spellings and talk about the different ways in which sounds can be represented by graphemes. The children could go on to work independently to write some sentences themselves.
2*(second): Ask the children to use dictionaries to help them to write alliterative sentences. Discuss the different possible initial graphemes for different sounds. Some pairs of children from Group 2 could use the computer for this activity.
3: Provide the children with the set of cards of adjectives and children's names and ask them to make as many alliterative phrases as they can and to write these down.

### Conclusion

Ask Group 2 to read aloud some of their alliterative sentences. Write some on the board or flip chart and discuss spellings. Encourage the children to read with intonation and expression and to pay attention to any punctuation as they do.

### Introduction and whole-class skills work

Begin the lesson by reading aloud a selection of tongue-twisters and alliterative sentences. Ask the children if they can remember what is special about the sentences. Try some of the traditional ones such as:

*Round the rugged rocks the ragged rascals ran.*
*She sells sea shells on the sea shore.*

Show the children the sentences and ask them to look at them carefully and to identify the common graphemes and the phonemes which they make. Ask someone to suggest a two- or three-word beginning for an alliterative sentence and then work with the class to develop this into a longer sentence. Encourage the children to think of ways in which the sentence may be changed and improved and consider words which may be added to it. Discuss phonemes and graphemes with the children and use opportunities when different graphemes represent the same phoneme (for example 'f' in 'fish' and 'ph' in 'photograph') to make spelling teaching points.

### Differentiated group activities

1*(second): Produce alliterative sentences using dictionaries (as Group 2, Hour 1).
2*(first): Group reading of tongue-twisters (as Group 1, Hour 1).
3: Ask Group 3 to look at the alliterative phrases they produced in the previous lesson, and ask them to expand these to full alliterative sentences.

### Conclusion

Ask Group 3 to read some of their alliterative sentences to the rest of the class. Write some of these on the board and discuss the correspondence between phonemes and graphemes. Begin to create a display of alliterative phrases and sentences and invite the children to add to it. They may do this partly by asking parents to tell them more well-known tongue-twisters.

**Note:** A third lesson could be produced if further alliterative poems are introduced. Children could go on to write their own poems and to use dictionaries to add to the collection of alliterative phrases and sentences on display.

# ADJECTIVES

| | | | |
|---|---|---|---|
| happy | astonishing | young | funny |
| jolly | clever | smiling | skilful |
| great | bright | delightful | excellent |
| interesting | lovely | marvellous | helpful |
| perfect | tidy | wonderful | kind |

# JACK AND THE BEANSTALK

## OBJECTIVES

| UNIT | SPELLING AND VOCABULARY | GRAMMAR AND PUNCTUATION | COMPREHENSION AND COMPOSITION |
|------|------|------|------|
| READING FICTION 'Jack and the Beanstalk'. | Learn new words linked to a story. | Turn statements into questions. Understand the use of question marks and other punctuation. | Retell a story using a flow chart. |

## ORGANIZATION (3 HOURS)

| | INTRODUCTION | WHOLE-CLASS SKILLS WORK | DIFFERENTIATED GROUP ACTIVITIES | CONCLUSION |
|------|------|------|------|------|
| **HOUR 1** | Shared reading of 'Jack and the Beanstalk'. Discussion about punctuation. | Raise awareness of punctuation through close textual examination. Look at the spelling of unfamiliar words. | 1: Re-read with expression. Prepare to read to an audience. 2: Read text and identify main incidents. 3*: Identify punctuation marks. | Select pupils from Group 1 to read to the rest of the class. Discuss the main incidents in the story identified by Group 2. |
| **HOUR 2** | Shared re-reading of 'Jack and the Beanstalk'. Shared writing of additional text. | Shared writing and focus upon punctuation. Turn statements into questions. | 1: Write additional text. Proofread own work. 2*: Guided re-reading with expression. Prepare to read to an audience. 3: Read text and identify main incidents. | Discussion about story endings and use of punctuation. |
| **HOUR 3** | Shared re-reading of 'Jack and the Beanstalk'. Discuss questions about the text. | | 1: Take statements from the text and turn into questions. 2: Identify punctuation marks. 3*: Guided re-reading with expression. Prepare to read to an audience. | Discussion of Group 1's questions and reinforcement through board work. |

## RESOURCES

Photocopiable pages 146 and 147 ('Jack and the Beanstalk – 1'), photocopiable page 148 ('Jack and the Beanstalk – 2'), Blu-Tack (or small Post-It notes), board or flip chart, OHP and acetate (optional), highlighter pens or coloured pens of different colours, writing materials. A copy of Roald Dahl's *Revolting Rhymes* (ISBN 0-14-050423-0, Puffin Books) would be useful.

## PREPARATION

Prepare sufficient copies of photocopiable pages 146 and 147 ('Jack and the Beanstalk – 1') and photocopiable page 148 ('Jack and the Beanstalk – 2') for each child to have one. Prepare an enlarged copy or OHT of photocopiable pages 146 and 147. Prepare an enlarged copy or OHT of photocopiable page 148 and cover all of the punctuation marks with small pieces of Blu-Tack (or Post-It notes). Have ready plenty of paper for the children to write their story endings on.

### Introduction and whole-class skills work

Show the children an enlarged copy or OHT of photocopiable page 148 ('Jack and the Beanstalk – 2') with the punctuation marks covered with Blu-Tack. Ask someone to read the story aloud. When the story has been read, ask the children if they can tell what the Blu-Tack is covering. Now re-read the first part of the story with them and ask them to suggest which punctuation marks might be missing. Reveal the punctuation gradually and discuss the nature of the punctuation and its purpose. Encourage them to use clues which are provided by the text. For example, you might ask questions such as:

- How do you know that this word does not begin a sentence?
- How do you know that there must be speech marks there?
- What tells you that we need a full stop there?

Now read the longer story aloud from photocopiable pages 146 and 147 ('Jack and the Beanstalk – 1') and ask the children to follow the text on an enlarged copy or OHT. Ask them to raise their hands whenever they think you have come to a full stop. Read the story once more and ask if they can tell where there is an example of speech. Show them the enlarged copy of the incomplete story again (photocopiable page 148) and ask them to look carefully at the speech marks.

There are some apostrophes in the story. These could be discussed if the children ask about them, and you may wish to talk about them during the group work session. As you read the story discuss any words with which the children are unfamiliar and help them to learn to read and spell them.

### Differentiated group activities

1: Provide the children with copies of photocopiable page 146 and 147 ('Jack and the Beanstalk – 1') and ask them to re-read the story with expression. Encourage them to take careful note of the punctuation when doing so. They should then prepare to read to an audience.

2: Provide the children with copies of photocopiable page 146 and 147 and ask them to re-read the story, identifying the main incidents as they do. Ask the children to make a list or a flow chart when they do so, but encourage them to write complete sentences with capital letters and full stops. Pairs of children from Group 2 could use the computer for this activity.

3*: Provide the children with copies of photocopiable page 148 ('Jack and the Beanstalk – 2'). Go through the text with them and ask them to explain each punctuation mark and its usage. Discuss apostrophes with them if you feel they are able to understand their use at this stage. The apostrophe which is used to abbreviate 'let us' into 'let's' may be a starting point for discussing other familiar words such as 'don't', 'doesn't' and 'wouldn't' (this is the 'elisive apostrophe').

### Conclusion

Ask each group to tell the rest of the class about the work they have been doing. Group 1 should have an opportunity to read the story aloud and the others should discuss the way in which the children used the punctuation marks to guide their reading. Note on the board or flip chart, the main incidents in the story as identified by Group 2.

### Introduction and whole-class skills work

Begin by re-reading the longer story on photocopiable pages 146 and 147 ('Jack and the Beanstalk – 1') with the children. Discuss the plot and then explain that you want the children to help you to write a different ending for the story. You could introduce the idea of a different version by reading the one which appears in Roald Dahl's *Revolting Rhymes*.

As you write the new ending of the story on the board or flip chart, encourage children to help you with punctuation as well as with ideas. Talk about the reasons for using full stops, commas and capital letters and, if they occur, speech marks.

### Differentiated group activities

1: Ask the children to write their own versions of the ending of the story. Encourage the children to use a checklist to proofread their work. This might be made up of a few simple questions such as:

*Have you put a capital letter at the beginning of each sentence?*
*Does each sentence end with a full stop?*
*Have you used commas to separate items in lists?*

The list itself may be used to remind children about the use of question marks in interrogative sentences. Pairs of children from Group 1 could use the computer for this activity.

2*: Re-read the story and prepare to read to an audience (as Group 1, Hour 1).

3: Re-read the story and identify the main incidents. Present these in list of flow chart form (as Group 2, Hour 1).

### Conclusion

Ask Group 1 to read their story endings to the class. Do the class agree with where the punctuation has been placed? Some children from Group 2 should have an opportunity to read the story to the class.

### Introduction and whole-class skills work

Re-read the shorter story on photocopiable page 148 with the children's help and then explain that you want them to help you to make up some questions about it. Begin with the first sentence:

> *Once upon a time there was a boy named Jack who lived with his mother in a little house near the woods.*

Ask the children to help you to write a question to go with the sentence. This might be: *Where did Jack live?* or *Who lived with Jack?* Go on to look at other sentences and to make up further questions. Show the children that the question sentences need to begin with a capital letter and end with a question mark.

### Differentiated group activities

1: Ask the group to select positive statements from the story and turn them into questions. Once again, a checklist maybe a useful device to promote proofreading. Pairs of children from Group 1 could use the computer for this activity.

2: Provide the children with copies of the longer story on photocopiable pages 146 and 147 and ask them to identify the punctuation marks. They should then underline or highlight commas, full stops, question marks and speech marks in different colours.

3*: Provide the children with copies of the complete story and read through it with them. Ask children to take turns reading the text, paying particular attention to the punctuation. They might each read successive sentences or they could read different characters, one child reading Jack's words, another his mother's and another the little man's. The other children could then read all the other text between them. Encourage them to notice speech marks and to understand their function.

### Conclusion

Discuss questions with the children and ask Group 1 to read some of theirs aloud. Write some on the board or flip chart and discuss the punctuation. Ask Group 3 to read aloud to the class.

# JACK AND THE BEANSTALK – 1

Once upon a time there was a boy named Jack who lived with his mother in a little house near the woods. They had very little money and they hardly had anything to eat except the potatoes and carrots which grew in their tiny field, and the butter and cheese which Jack's mother made from the milk which Daisy, their cow, gave.

Things were so bad that one day Jack's mother told him to go to the nearest town and sell the cow so that they would be able to buy more food.

"But if I sell the cow, we won't have any milk or butter or cheese," said Jack.

"Don't argue with me, young man!" said his mother crossly. "You just get your coat on and go to the town and sell Daisy."

Jack knew better than to argue with his mother, so he got ready and found a rope to lead Daisy along the road.

"Make sure you get plenty of money for her!" called his mother as Jack set off down the road.

"I'll do my best," Jack replied and he waved as he turned the corner and headed for the town.

Jack had only walked for a mile when Daisy decided she did not want to walk any further and sat down in the road. Jack could not get her to move and so he sat down next to her and waited for her to decide to get up.

# JACK AND THE BEANSTALK – 1
## (CONTINUED)

Suddenly he heard a voice. He looked round and saw a little man wearing a green hat and a green suit.

"Where are you taking that cow?" asked the man.

"I'm taking her to the town to sell her," replied Jack. "We need the money to buy food."

"I'll buy her!" said the man with a smile. "And I'll give you something much better than money for her."

"What do you mean?" asked Jack.

"I'll give you something which will help to make you rich so that you'll never need to be hungry again." The little man held out three dried beans and said, "Here, take these for your cow. They are magic beans and I promise they will help you to make a fortune."

Jack thought about what the man had said. He could not get Daisy to move and so he could not take her to town to sell her anyway. Even if he did sell her he knew he would only get a few pounds because she was a very old cow. If he took the magic beans he might make himself and his mother rich.

"I'll take them!" he said and he handed the man the lead and put the beans in his pocket. "Just wait until I tell Mum what I got for Daisy!" he cried. "She'll be so pleased with me I bet she'll make me my favourite supper!"

# JACK AND THE BEANSTALK – 2

Once upon a time there was a boy named Jack who lived with his mother in a little house near the woods. They had very little money and they hardly had anything to eat except the potatoes and carrots which grew in their tiny field, and the butter and cheese which Jack's mother made from the milk which Daisy, their cow, gave.

Things were so bad that one day Jack's mother told him to go to the nearest town and sell the cow so that they would be able to buy more food.

"But if I sell the cow, we won't have any milk or butter or cheese," said Jack.

"Don't argue with me, young man!" said his mother crossly. "You just get your coat on and go to the town and sell Daisy."

Jack knew better than to argue with his mother, so he got ready and found a rope to lead Daisy along the road.

# MRS LEACH AND THE LEAKS

## OBJECTIVES

| UNIT | SPELLING AND VOCABULARY | GRAMMAR AND PUNCTUATION | COMPREHENSION AND COMPOSITION |
|---|---|---|---|
| READING FICTION 'Mrs Leach and the Leaks'. | Discriminate, read and spell the phonemes ea (long as in hear) and ea (short as in head). Identify other ways in which the digraph ea may be sounded in commonly used words. | Read text aloud with intonation and expression appropriate to the grammar and punctuation. | Reinforce and apply word level skills through shared and guided reading. |

## ORGANIZATION (3 HOURS)

| | INTRODUCTION | WHOLE-CLASS SKILLS WORK | DIFFERENTIATED GROUP ACTIVITIES | CONCLUSION |
|---|---|---|---|---|
| HOUR 1 | Shared reading of 'Mrs Leach and the Leaks'. | Raise phonological awareness by drawing attention to the different ways in which the digraph ea can be pronounced. | 1*(first): Re-read with expression. Prepare to read to an audience. Make notes on an ending to the story. 2*(second): Read and identify words containing the digraph ea. 3: Explore rhyming words containing the digraph ea. | Group 1 to re-read to the rest of the class, which should follow and look out for words containing the digraph ea. Discuss the different ways in which ea may be pronounced. |
| HOUR 2 | Look at words that include the digraph ea. Write sentences that include the words. Sort them into groups. | Discriminate between the common pronunciations of the digraph ea. | 1: Read and identify words containing the digraph ea. Use notes to write a continuation of the story. 2*: Explore rhyming words containing the digraph ea. 3: Re-read with expression. Prepare to read to an audience. | Group 2 to give examples of rhyming words containing the digraph ea. Discuss these. |
| HOUR 3 | Shared use of cards with words containing the digraph ea as starting point to writing sentences. | Shared activity using words containing the digraph ea on cards. | 1: Find words containing the digraph ea in reading books. Sort them by pronunciation. 2*: Guided reading. Identify words containing the digraph ea. 3: Write sentences including words that contain the digraph ea. | Use cards to match words containing the digraph ea. Discuss their pronunciation. |

## RESOURCES

Photocopiable page 152 ('EA words'), photocopiable page 153 ('Mrs Leach and the Leaks'), some examples of words which include the digraph 'ea' written on the board, a set of word cards (sufficient for at least one for each member of the class), the children's reading books, board or flip chart, highlighter pens, writing materials.

### PREPARATION

Prepare an enlarged copy or OHT of photocopiable page 153 as well as sufficient individual copies for each child to use. Make a set of cards on which have been written words containing the digraph 'ea' from photocopiable page 152. Write other words containing 'ea' on the board or flip chart.

### Introduction and whole-class skills work

**Note:** The vowel digraph 'ea' may be pronounced in different ways in the words which children commonly meet during Year 2. The National Literacy Strategy requires you to help children to discriminate between the 'ea' in 'head' and the 'ea' in 'hear'. To concentrate solely on these two pronunciations would be to deny children knowledge of other common pronunciations, so this activity includes other common 'ea' words with other phonemes – for example, 'break' and 'early'.

Read the text on photocopiable page 153 ('Mrs Leach and the Leaks') to the children. Ask them to look at an enlargement or OHT of the text as you re-read it and to identify words that include the digraph 'ea'. Ask the children about the words.

Look for examples such as 'lead' and 'read', which have alternative pronunciations according to their meanings. Show these words to the children in different sentences to emphasize that they need to use semantic cues to help them in their reading.

For example:

> *The pipes were made from lead.*
> *Sue took the lead in the egg and spoon race.*
> *I like to read comics.*
> *I have read many comics.*

### Differentiated group activities

1*(first): Give each child a copy of photocopiable page 153 and ask them to re-read the story with expression. They should then prepare to read to an audience. They should go on to make notes on an ending for the story. Explain that they will be using the notes in the next lesson as a starting point for writing a story ending. Some pairs of children from Group 1 could use the computer to make their notes for this activity.

2*(second): Give each child a copy of photocopiable page 153 and ask them to re-read the story. Ask them to identify words with the digraph 'ea' in them and to underline or highlight them..

3: Give each child a copy of photocopiable page 152. Ask them to identify the words in which the vowel sounds match and to underline or highlight them. This might include medial vowel sounds as in 'read' and 'real' and rhymes such as 'head' and 'bread'.

### Conclusion

Ask Group 1 to read the story aloud and ask other children to follow and look out for words containing the digraph 'ea'. Discuss the different ways in which 'ea' may be pronounced in different words.

### Introduction and whole-class skills work

Re-read the story 'Mrs Leach and the Leaks' with the children and ask them to read it from an enlarged copy or OHT and find the words containing the digraph 'ea'. Write the words 'head', 'each', 'early' and 'break' on the board or flip chart as headings for four lists and ask the children to look through the story and find each 'ea' word and suggest which heading it should be written under. When they have done this, introduce some 'ea' words which do not appear in the story and read them with the children and then ask them to assign them to the correct lists according to pronunciation. The following words could be used:

| | | |
|---|---|---|
| search | steak | ready |
| fear | earth | tear[1] |

[1] Note that 'tear' has two pronunciations. You could introduce an additional pronunciation by showing the children 'heart' and 'hearth'.

### Differentiated group activities

1: Identify words containing the digraph 'ea' (as Group 2, Hour 1). Ask the children to use their notes from the previous lesson to write a continuation of the story. Some pairs of children from Group 1 could use the computer to write their stories.

2*(second): Explore rhyming words containing 'ea' (as Group 3, Hour 1).

3*(first): Re-read with expression. Prepare to read to an audience (as Group 1, Hour 1).

### Conclusion

Ask Groups 1 and 2 to tell the rest of the class about the rhyming words which they found and make a list of these on the board or flip chart showing the different ways in which 'ea' may be pronounced. Select children form Group 1 to read out their story endings.

### Introduction and whole-class skills work

Give each child a card with a word which includes the digraph 'ea' (you might like to use photocopiable page 152 for this purpose). Ask the children to read their words aloud in turn and help anyone who is unable to do so. Next, write an 'ea' word on the board and ask children who have words which include 'ea' pronounced in the same way as in the word on the board to hold their cards up. For example, if you held up the word 'head', children with 'dead', 'dread', 'ahead' should hold up their cards.

Discuss with the children the words such as 'read' and 'lead' which have alternative pronunciations and tell children with those words that they may hold their cards up more than once. The activity should give you an opportunity to check on individuals' understanding of the correspondence between graphemes and phonemes.

### Differentiated group activities

1: Provide the children with a selection of reading books and ask them to find words containing the digraph 'ea' in them. Ask them to write another sentence containing each word, to show that they have understood its meaning .

2*: Re-read the story 'Mrs Leach and the Leaks' to the children. Provide them with copies and ask them to identify words containing the digraph 'ea'. Use the opportunity to write some of the words on the board or flip chart and discuss their spellings.

3: Ask the group to write sentences which include 'ea' words. They should use the list provided on photocopiable page 152 as a word bank. Some pairs of children from Group 3 could use the computer for this activity.

### Conclusion

Give out the cards with 'ea' words written on them so that each child has one. Write words on the board or flip chart which include the digraph 'ea' and ask the children to hold their word up if it has the same phoneme for 'ea' as the word you are holding. Children could be asked to make a collection of further 'ea' words at home with the help of parents and other adults.

# *EA* WORDS

| | | | | |
|---|---|---|---|---|
| hear | reach | knead | steak | treat | ahead |
| bread | teach | ear | tear | each | seat |
| near | dread | real | search | tease | yeast |
| head | beard | dear | early | bean | beach |
| dead | idea | read | wear | easy | bead |
| lead | break | please | leak | pea | fear |

# MRS LEACH AND THE LEAKS

I reached school quite early yesterday. My teacher was busy in the classroom. She was wearing a really old coat and on her head was a green hat.

"Please could you help me?" she asked. "There is a leak in the roof."

"Oh dear!" I replied.

"Don't stand too near or the drips of water will fall on your head."

I helped my teacher to put buckets under the leaks, but each one filled so quickly that I had to keep emptying them.

"This is not easy, is it?" she said. "I think we had better get the headteacher. I can't leave the room or we'll have a flood. Please would you go and find him, Jade?"

I went off to search for Mr Dean, the headteacher, and found him in his office. "What do you want, dear?" he asked.

I told him about the leaking roof and about Mrs Leach and the buckets.

Mr Dean asked me to find Mrs Mears, the caretaker, and he rushed off to help Mrs Leach.

When Mrs Mears and I got to the classroom, Mr Dean and Mrs Leach were emptying buckets into the sink as soon as each one filled up.

"This is dreadful!" said Mrs Mears. She looked at the water leaking through the ceiling and at the

buckets on the floor. Outside the rain was pouring down.

"We don't have enough buckets for all the leaks," said Mr Dean.

"I have an idea!" said Mrs Mears, and she asked me to go with her to the nursery to help her to carry something.

# FACT OR FICTION?

## OBJECTIVES

| UNIT | SPELLING AND VOCABULARY | GRAMMAR AND PUNCTUATION | COMPREHENSION AND COMPOSITION |
|---|---|---|---|
| READING AND WRITING NON-FICTION 'Animals' and 'Fact or Fiction?' | Learn new words related to a topic. Discuss spelling and sounds. Use synonyms to aid understanding of new words. | Write in clear sentences using capital letters, full stops and question marks accurately. | Understand the distinction between fact and fiction. Pose questions and record them in writing. Scan a text and look for key words and phrases and sub-headings. |

## ORGANIZATION (5 HOURS)

| | INTRODUCTION | WHOLE-CLASS SKILLS WORK | DIFFERENTIATED GROUP ACTIVITIES | CONCLUSION |
|---|---|---|---|---|
| HOUR 1 | Shared reading of 'Animals'. Discussion about its content. | Look at new words and discuss pronunciation. Introduction to synonyms. | 1: Re-read text and complete 'Fact or Fiction?' sheet. 2*: Re-read and discuss 'Animals' text. Make up questions about it. 3: Re-read 'Animals' and find key words. | Discuss the terms fact and fiction. Ask children to make up sentences orally which may be fact or fiction. |
| HOUR 2 | Shared re-reading of 'Animals'. Discussion about its headings. | Introduction to proper nouns. Look at the pronunciation of some of the animals' names. | 1*: Write additional text using appropriate headings. 2: Re-read text and complete 'Fact or Fiction?' sheet. 3: Identify proper nouns and other words in the text which begin with capital letters. | Examine spelling and pronunciation of proper nouns. Make notes with the class under sub-headings. |
| HOUR 3 | Discussion about fact and fiction based upon statements on the 'Fact or Fiction?' photocopiable. | Introduction to antonyms. Discussion about the 'Fact or Fiction?' text. | 1*(second): Write factual and fictional sentences related to the 'Animals' text. 2: Write additional text using appropriate headings. 3*(first): Guided writing of factual and fictional text. | Group 3 to show the rest of the class the factual/ fictional statements they have written. Discussion about the antonyms work done by Group 1. |
| HOUR 4 | Look at the text of 'Animals'. Make up questions to go with it. | Look at sentence structures. Shared writing using capital letters, full stops and question marks. | 1: Re-read and discuss 'Animals' text. Make up questions about it. 2*(first): Guided writing of factual and fictional text. 3*(second): Further writing of factual and fictional text. | Answer questions written by Group 1. Pose further questions orally. |
| HOUR 5 | Shared examination of other texts about animals and writing information together. | Learn to spell new words related to topic. | 1*(first): Guided writing of further information about animals based upon other texts. 2: Re-read and discuss 'Animals' text. Make up questions about it. 3*(second): Make notes from simple texts about animals. | Discuss new information on animals. Learn spellings related to topic. |

## RESOURCES
Photocopiable pages 159 and 160 ('Animals'), photocopiable page 161 ('Fact or Fiction?'), examples of other texts (varying in standards of difficulty) about animals, pictures of animals from magazines, examples of any text with sub-headings, board or flip chart, writing materials. A dictionary of synonyms and a dictionary of antonyms may be useful for the teacher to refer to.

## PREPARATION
Make an enlarged copy or OHT of photocopiabloe pages 159 and 160 ('Animals') and sufficient copies for each child to have one. Do the same for photocopiable page 161 ('Fact or Fiction?'). Make a collection of pictures of and text about animals, taken from newspapers and magazines to display on walls, on an OHP and to pass around the class. Make an enlarged copy or OHT of a piece of simple text that contains sub-headings.

### Introduction and whole-class skills work
Write the words 'fact', 'fiction' and 'non-fiction' on the board or flip chart and ask the children to help you to make lists of things which are facts, and texts which are fiction and non-fiction. Ask questions such as:

*Is it a fact that a girl called Goldilocks ate some bears' porridge?*
*What kind of book would you read about fairies in?*
*What kind of book would give you information about France?*

Show the children an enlarged copy or OHT of photocopiable pages 159 and 160 ('Animals') and ask them to look at it carefully. Ask them if it is a story or a poem or something else. Ask them to tell you whether they think it is factual or fiction and discuss these terms with the children.

Read 'Animals' with the children and discuss the content and some of the vocabulary. Many of the types of animal may be unfamiliar to the children but you might bring in pictures from advertisements to show them what the animals look like. They will probably also need help with words like:

| | | |
|---|---|---|
| *fierce* | *Australia* | *countries* |
| *usually* | *enormous* | *museums* |
| *extinct* | *particular* | *environment* |

Write the words on the board or flip chart and talk about them. Show the children how they can break the words into syllables to enable them to read them. In order to explain the meanings of the words, it may be useful to provide synonyms and match these to the words. For example:

*types – kinds*    *habitat – home*    *diet – food*

### Differentiated group activities
1: Give the children copies of photocopiable page 161 ('Fact or Fiction?') and ask them to read the text and answer the questions.
2*: Give the children copies of photocopiable pages 159 and 160 ('Animals') and ask them to re-read it with you. Talk about any difficult words and then ask them to make up questions orally.
3: Provide the children with a list of words from the text 'Animals' and ask them to read through the text and try to find the words. As they do so, they should copy the words carefully and, if possible, write sentences which include them.

### Conclusion
Talk with the children about the things they have discovered from the text. Look again at the terms 'fact' and 'fiction' and ask the children to make up statements about animals which are factual and fictional.

### Introduction and whole-class skills work

Discuss some of the terms which children encountered in the previous lesson. In particular, reinforce the concepts of 'fact', 'fiction' and 'non-fiction'.

Look together at the enlarged copy or OHT of 'Animals' with the children once again and talk about the way the text is set out. Talk about sub-headings and their purpose. Show the children enlarged copies of some other texts which include headings and discuss these too.

Look with the children at some of the proper nouns in the text and discuss the use of capital letters and the spellings. Most of the place names are simple and phonically regular. Others may be regular in their country of origin but may present problems for English speakers.

### Differentiated group activities

1*: Ask this group to make notes about other facts which they know about animals and then write about these under appropriate headings. They may use page 160 for this.
2: Ask the children to re-read the text 'Animals' and then give them photocopies of photocopiable page 161 ('Fact or Fiction?'). Ask them to answer the questions.
3: Ask the children to skim through their copies of the 'Animals' text and to identify the proper nouns. They should then write these down. Encourage them to look carefully at the text and identify words with capital letters and then determine whether these are proper nouns or words which begin sentences.

### Conclusion

Write on the board or flip chart the names of the animals and countries that appear in the 'Animals' text. Discuss their spelling and pronunciation. Write out the headings used in the text, as well as any new ones the children may suggest. For example, you could use headings such as 'Mammals' and then write sentences based upon information in the text and other information provided by the children, such as how many mammals are common pets.

### Introduction and whole-skills work

Discuss again with the children the terms 'fact' and 'fiction'. Explain what the words mean and suggest some statements which are factual or fictional. Group 1 will already have done some work on fact and fiction and should be asked to explain what they did.

Look at the enlarged copy or OHT of photocopiable page 161 ('Fact or Fiction?') with the children and ask them to make up some additional statements. Write these on the board or flip chart and ask the children if they are fact or fiction, or true or false. Make up some questions with the children about the 'Animals' text and ask them which are factual and which fictional.

Talk with the children about antonyms when the opportunity arises. For example, you could use statements which include antonyms such as:

*The most unpopular animals in Britain are the dog and the cat.*
*Lions are shy but mice are very fierce.*

Discuss the spellings of the antonyms and talk about the way in which some opposites are created simply by adding a prefix. This should be related to the 'Swimming after school' unit from Term 2.

### Differentiated group activities

1*(second): Ask the children to write sentences which are factual and fictional related to the text 'Animals'. Emphasize that they should look at some key adjectives and change these to enable them to write sentences with meanings opposite to those in the text.
2: Writing additional text using headings (as Group 1, Hour 2).
3*(first): Ask the children to write some factual and some fictional sentences. Discuss the difference. Encourage the children to check their spelling and punctuation.

### Conclusion

Show the rest of the class the fact or fiction statements written with Group 3 and ask the children to decide which are true and which untrue. Discuss some of the antonyms used by Group 1 and show the children how these are spelled.

### Introduction and whole-class skills work

Look again at the 'Animals' text and ask the children to read it with you from the enlarged copy or OHT. Ask them to think of some questions to go with the text and write these down on the board or flip chart. Encourage the children to use capital letters and question marks accurately.

In order to prompt the children, you may need to ask them to pick out different subjects from the text and then help to record possible questions using a spider chart. Write the subject of the questions in the middle of the board and then ask the children to think of things which could be asked about it. Record these around the subject word. For example:

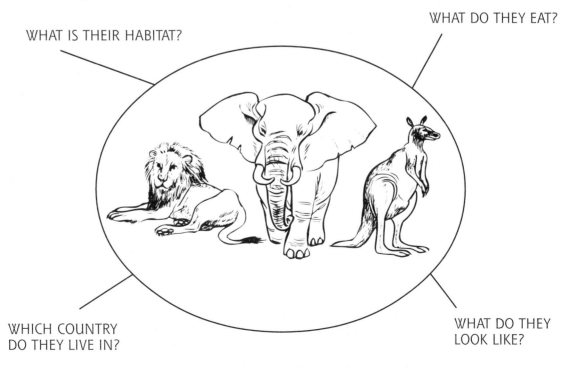

WHAT DO THEY EAT?

WHAT IS THEIR HABITAT?

WHICH COUNTRY
DO THEY LIVE IN?

WHAT DO THEY
LOOK LIKE?

Choose one of these questions to answer and show the children the correct way in which to write a complete answer – *Sheep and pigs are types of farm animal.*

### Differentiated group activities

1: Ask the children to read the 'Animals' text and to make up questions related to it. They could be set a target of writing ten questions or you could ask them to make up two questions for each heading in the text. Ask the children to provide the answers on a separate sheet.

2*(first): Writing factual and fictional sentences (as Group 3, Hour 3).

3*(second): Ask the children to follow up the work they did with you in the previous lesson by independently writing sentences which are true or false. You may need to work with the children after a few minutes to provide support.

### Conclusion

Display the enlarged version or OHT of 'Animals' and ask Group 1 to read aloud some of their questions and ask the class to use the text to answer them.

### Introduction and whole-class skills work

Use the final lesson in the series to revise some of the concepts learned in the previous ones by showing the children some other texts about animals and discussing them. Talk about whether the information given is true or false or opinion. Discuss the purpose of the different texts and show some enlarged versions to illustrate the use of headings and layout.

Show the children some of the words which they have learned during the series of lessons and cover each in turn and ask the children to help you to spell them correctly.

### Differentiated group activities

1*(first): Provide the children with some of the examples of writing about animals and ask them to find further information and to write about it using headings. Encourage the children to skim and scan the texts to find out what information they provide.

2: Write questions about the 'Animals' text (as Group 1, Hour 4).

3*(second): Provide the children with some of the simpler texts on animals and ask them to look at them and to make a note of any interesting things which they discover.

### Conclusion

Discuss the new information on animals which Groups 1 and 3 have found and recorded. Look again at the spellings and help the children to learn them. Again, the information discovered could be presented in grid form as on page 160.

You may wish to conclude the series of lessons with a quiz in which you provide some definitions orally of the words and concepts which children have encountered. For example:

- Which word describes books which contain stories?
- Which word means the place where something lives?
- Which word means well-liked?
- Which word means that something is true: fact, fiction or opinion?

# ANIMALS

## THE FIRST ANIMALS

The first animals that we know much about lived 200 million years ago and many of them were enormous. We call these animals 'dinosaurs' and you can sometimes see their bones in museums. Although they were so huge, most of them were not fierce and did not eat other animals. They had all died out, or become extinct, many years before the first humans appeared in the world.

## UNUSUAL ANIMALS

There are some animals which you would think were made up if you had never seen one before. The platypus, which lives in Australia, is furry and has four legs, but it has a beak like a duck's and it lays eggs. What about a bird taller than a human, which eats stones, lays eggs the size of rugby balls, runs at 60 miles an hour, and can't fly? That's the African ostrich!

# ANIMALS (CONTINUED)

## FARM ANIMALS

In this country, farms are one of the places where we can still see many kinds of animals. Sheep, pigs, cows and horses can be seen in fields in many parts of the country and we are often able to visit farms to see the animals grow and learn about the part they play and how they are useful to humans. Birds are animals too, of course, and we see chickens, ducks and geese on many farms.

■ You can set out the information you have discovered on animals in this grid.

| NAME OF ANIMAL | TYPE OF ANIMAL | HABITAT | COUNTRY |
|---|---|---|---|
|  |  |  |  |
|  |  |  |  |
|  |  |  |  |
|  |  |  |  |
|  |  |  |  |
|  |  |  |  |
|  |  |  |  |

# FACT OR FICTION?

■ Which of these statements is fact and which is fiction? Can you write a true statement for each of the sentences which you think is untrue?

■ Write some statements of your own for your friends to decide if they are fact or fiction?

|  | FACT | FICTION |
|---|---|---|
| You can still see dinosaurs today in zoos. |  |  |
| All dinosaurs ate meat. |  |  |
| The platypus comes from Australia. |  |  |
| Ostriches are very good at flying. |  |  |
| Ostriches eat stones and lay large eggs. |  |  |
| Birds are not animals. |  |  |
| Chickens, ducks and geese are all types of bird. |  |  |
| Polar bears live in the African jungle. |  |  |
| Giraffes have stripes to help them to hide in the jungle. |  |  |
| Tigers eat leaves from the tops of trees. |  |  |

# INDEXES

## OBJECTIVES

| UNIT | SPELLING AND VOCABULARY | GRAMMAR AND PUNCTUATION | COMPREHENSION AND COMPOSITION |
|---|---|---|---|
| READING NON-FICTION Indexes. | Learn new words related to a topic.<br>Secure reading and spelling of pupils' names. | Reinforce the use of commas in lists. | Examine a range of ordered texts.<br>Discuss how and why they are used.<br>Use an index to move around text. |

## ORGANIZATION (4 HOURS)

| | INTRODUCTION | WHOLE-CLASS SKILLS WORK | DIFFERENTIATED GROUP ACTIVITIES | CONCLUSION |
|---|---|---|---|---|
| **HOUR 1** | Shared reading of an index. | Look at new words and discriminate syllables. | 1: Use an index to find items in a book.<br>2*(first): Read and alphabetize words.<br>3*(second): Look at a range of reference materials and discuss how they should be used. | Look again at index and answer questions about it. Display a range of ordered texts. |
| **HOUR 2** | Shared re-reading of an index. | Match words and look closely at spellings. | 1*(second): Read and alphabetize words.<br>2: Look at a range of reference materials and discuss how they should be used.<br>3*(first): Use an index to find items in a book. | Alphabetize words that have the same initial letter. |
| **HOUR 3** | Shared examination of a range of ordered books. | Alphabetize names of children in class. | 1*(first): Use a simple text book to identify key words and place them in an index.<br>2: Use an index to find items in a book.<br>3*(second): Alphabetizing activity. | Discuss indexes produced by Group 1. |
| **HOUR 4** | Shared examination of catalogues with indexes. | Look up items in catalogues. | 1*: Look at a catalogue and make up questions for others.<br>2: Identify items in an index.<br>3: Look at a catalogue and find selected items. | Look again at photocopiable index and revise children's understanding of an index. |

## RESOURCES

Photocopiable page 166 (Catalogue Index), a range of catalogues (enough for two groups to use at once), such as those produced by mail order companies or catalogue showrooms, a set of word cards, some alphabetically ordered books such as dictionaries, telephone directories and encyclopædias, a selection of other simple reference books, a large chart showing the alphabet, board or flip chart, highlighter pens, coloured pens or pencils, writing materials.

## PREPARATION

Prepare an enlarged copy or OHT of photocopiable page 166 (Catalogue Index) as well as copies for every child in the class. Prepare a list of words from the index of one of the reference books and make sufficient copies for each of the children to have one (but do not present the words in alphabetical order). Make a set of cards with the children's names written on them and another set of cards of random words that the children will be able to alphabetize. Make copies of a piece of text from which the children will be able to pick key index entries. Display the alphabet chart near to the board or flip chart.

### Introduction and whole-class skills work

Show the children an enlarged copy or OHT of photocopiable page 166 (Catalogue Index) and ask them what they notice about it. Ask the following questions:

> *How would you read it?*
> *What order are the words placed in?*
> *What do the numbers tell us?*
> *Where might you find such a list?*
> *How would you use it?*

Write some of the index entries on the board or flip chart and ask the children to find them in the index. Encourage them to think about the structure of the words and to sound them out carefully in their heads before saying them aloud.

Next, explain that the numbers represent pages in a book and that they are separated by commas so that we can tell easily what they are. Ask questions such as: *On which pages would you find out about...?* and *Could you find out about...in this book?* Give some words which do, and some which do not, appear in the index.

### Differentiated group activities

1: Provide the group with multiple copies of a simple reference book and ask the children to use the index to find out about at least five items. Ask them to write a sentence about each.

2*(first): Provide the children with copies of a list of words (these could be taken from the index of the book used by Group 1) and ask the children to place the words in alphabetical order. Some pairs of children could use the computer for this activity.

3*(second): Provide the children with a range of ordered reference materials such as dictionaries, telephone directories and encyclopædias. Ask them to discuss how these are used and then to write a sentence explaining the purpose of each.

### Conclusion

Reinforce the concept of ordered text by referring to the index again. Show the class the books which Group 3 have been looking at and discuss their purpose. Add these books to a class display of ordered texts.

### Introduction and whole-class skills work

Begin by reminding the children about the work they were doing in the previous lesson and by showing them once more the enlarged copy of the index that they discussed.

You will need to ask many of the same questions again, but this time focus upon words which begin with the same letter. Ask the children if they can tell you why the words are ordered as they are and discuss the use of second and third letters and so on. Write some of the words on the board or flip chart and ask the children to look at the alphabet as they decide in which order the words should be placed.

When looking at the words which begin with 'c', ask the children if they can listen carefully as you read them aloud and tell you which word has a different initial sound for the others ('cycles' has a soft 'c' while the other words in this index, such as clocks, begin with a hard 'c').

### Differentiated group activities

1*(second): Alphabetizing activity (as Group 2, Hour 1).

2: Look at and discuss reference materials (as Group 3, Hour 1).

3*(first): Exercise using indexes (as Group 1, Hour 1). You may need to spend time with Group 3 while Group 1 read independently at first.

### Conclusion

Write some words on the board or flip chart that have the same initial letter and ask the children to help you to put them into alphabetical order using the second letters. Ask Group 1 to read some of their alphabetical lists and invite the class to check if they are correctly ordered.

### Introduction and whole-class skills work

Begin by reminding the children about previous work with indexes and reinforce the concept of alphabetical ordering using the second and third letters of words and so on. Show them once more the index which was discussed in the previous lesson.

Next, show the children some names of members of the class which have been written on card. Ask three children each to come out to the front and hold a word. Ask the others to suggest how the children should stand in alphabetical order from left to right. Repeat the exercise and try to use names which have first letters in common.

Show the children an enlarged copy or OHT of some simple text and read it to them while they follow it. Stop at the end of each page and ask the children to suggest which are the key words which should appear in an index and write these down. Ask the children to help you to sort the words into alphabetical order.

### Differentiated group activities

1*(first): Give each of the children a simple text book and ask them to identify key words and create an index. This is a development of the work which the group did in the first lesson in the unit. Encourage the children to scan the text and to look for important words. The words could be those which refer to pictures and these may provide clues for the children. Encourage them, in particular, to look for proper nouns and remind them

that these are used with capital letters.
2: Exercise using indexes (as Group 1, Hour 1).
3*(second): Give the children the set of cards with words on and ask them to place them in alphabetical order. Remind the children that they may need to look at second and third letters and so on. The children should have a selection of cards spread out face downwards in the centre of the table and they should each choose three or four at a time, turn them over, and then write them in alphabetical order. As they finish each group of words they should return them, face down, to the centre of the table so that others may use them too.

### Conclusion
Ask each group to tell the rest of the class about what they have learned about alphabetical order and indexes. Show the class the indexes which Group 1 have been making and discuss their purpose.

### Introduction and whole-class skills work
Give out copies of a catalogue so that children may share them in pairs or threes. Ask the children to find the index and explain that it is spread over more than one page. Write words, one at a time, on the board or flip chart and ask the children to find them in the index and tell you on which pages the items might be found.

When the children have become confident about their ability to find the words in the index, ask them to find some items in the catalogue. Take one letter section from the index and write the words on the board and ask the children why the words are arranged as they are. For example, in 'shirts', 'shoes', 'sports bags', 'swings', they might explain that 'shirts' comes before 'shoes' because 'i' which is the third letter in 'shirts' comes before 'o' which is the third letter in 'shoes'.

### Differentiated group activities
1*: Ask the children to look at the catalogues. Ask them to use the index and to make up questions such as: *Find the page which has calculators. What kind of calculator could you buy for less than £10?*
2: Provide the children with copies of photocopiable page 166 (Catalogue Index) and a separate list of words, many of which may be found in the photocopiable index. Ask them to highlight or underline the words in your list which also appear in the index and to do the same on the index. They could use a selection of different coloured pens or pencils to do this.
3: Provide the children with copies of the catalogue and a list of items. Ask them to use the index to find them in the catalogue. They could write down the catalogue number for the item or the price to show that they have done this.

### Conclusion
Ask each group to tell the rest of the class about the activities which they have been doing. Reinforce the concept of ordered text by referring to the index again. As this is the final lesson in the unit, ensure that the children fully understand how an index can help them to find information and that they understand the way in which words in an index are arranged in alphabetical order.

# CATALOGUE INDEX

# BOOK COVERS

## OBJECTIVES

| UNIT | SPELLING AND VOCABULARY | GRAMMAR AND PUNCTUATION | COMPREHENSION AND COMPOSITION |
|------|------|------|------|
| READING AND WRITING NON-FICTION Information from book covers. | Learn new words related to a topic. | Write in clear sentences using capital letters, full stops and question marks accurately. | Read about authors from information on book covers. Raise awareness of authorship and publication. |

## ORGANIZATION (2 HOURS)

| | INTRODUCTION | WHOLE-CLASS SKILLS WORK | DIFFERENTIATED GROUP ACTIVITIES | CONCLUSION |
|------|------|------|------|------|
| HOUR 1 | Shared examination of a book cover. | Look at some new words and discuss pronunciation. Learn to spell words such as *author, illustrator, publisher* and *cover*. | 1*(second): Look at a range of books and answer questions about the covers. 2*(first): Complete chart about book covers. 3: Make a book cover with title, author, etc. | Discuss book covers and look at further examples. |
| HOUR 2 | Look at display of the anatomy of a book. | Look at key words including *contents, chapter, index, fiction* and *non-fiction*. | 1*(second): Look at another range of books and sort them into types. 2*(first): Make a book cover with title, author, etc. 3: Complete chart about book covers. | Look at Group 1's sort and at the chart completed by Groups 2 and 3. Look again at the anatomy of a book. |

## RESOURCES

Photocopiable page 169 (Finding Information from Book Covers), several books at an appropriate reading level for the children, a display of the anatomy of a book (see below), Post-It notes or card for labelling the display, paper, coloured pencils, writing materials.

## PREPARATION

Make enough copies of photocopiable page 169 for each child in Groups 2 and 3 to have one. Make a display of the anatomy of a book: this can be created by taking a book which is damaged and cutting it up so that the cover (front and back), the title page, contents, publisher's information page and so on can be displayed with labels on card or Post-It notes. Have ready plenty of paper for Groups 2 and 3 to do book design work on.

### Introduction and whole-class skills work

Show the children a book (preferably a Big Book) and ask them what the cover tells them about the book and its contents. Discuss with them how readers, including adults, are often drawn to books by their covers and explain that it is not only the bright colours and pictures which attract them. Look at, and discuss, the back cover too.

Discuss the information provided by the cover, especially the following:
- author
- title
- publisher
- illustrator/photographer
- price

Explain that we can also find information about the year in which the book was published by looking inside. Look at the words above with the children and help them to learn to spell them by discussing syllables and phoneme/grapheme relationships. Look, in particular, at the endings of 'author', 'illustrator' and 'publisher' and explain that a similar sound can be represented by different graphemes.

### Differentiated group activities

1*(second): Provide this group with a selection of books or with access to a library or reading corner and ask the children to look at the books and answer questions about them as they look at the covers. They might be asked the following for each book:

- What is the title?
- Who is the author?
- Which company published the book?
- What do you think the book is about?
- Is the book fictional or non-fictional?

2*(first): Provide the children with copies of photocopiable page 169 and a selection of books. Ask them to complete the grid with the relevant details. Encourage the children to use capital letters and full stops accurately.

3: Provide the children with paper and coloured pencils and ask them to design a book cover for one of their favourite books. They should include a title, author, illustrator and publisher and should show an awareness of the ways in which these are presented to catch the reader's eye.

### Conclusion

Look with the children at some of the book covers which Group 3 have designed and at some from books in the classroom. Draw the children's attention to some of the other features of book covers such as the blurb and notes about the author. Look again at the spellings of key words.

### Introduction and whole-class skills work

Show the children the display of the anatomy of a book. Ask them to think about some of the words which they learned in the previous lesson and ask children to come out and point to the author's name and so forth. Discuss the way in which you have labelled the display and talk about the different parts of a book.

Talk with the children about the book and ask them if they think it is a fiction book or a non-fiction book. Ask them to explain their answers and then show them other books and ask children to inspect them and then explain to the rest of the class what they could find by looking at the cover and at other key pages. Look at the spellings of the words 'index', 'contents', 'fiction', 'non-fiction' and at other words learned in the previous lesson.

### Differentiated group activities

1*(second): Ask the children to look at a different range of books and to sort them into different types. Encourage the children to create their own categories at first but intervene to discuss these and to suggest others. These might include:

- stories
- poetry books
- reference books
- directories

2*(first): Book cover design activity (as Group 3, Hour 1).
3: Complete chart about book covers (as Group 2, Hour 1).

### Conclusion

Ask Group 1 to show the others how they sorted their books and discuss the categories with the whole class. Look at the charts which Groups 2 and 3 have completed and discuss these. Finally, look again at the display of the anatomy of a book and revise the names of the different parts.

# FINDING INFORMATION FROM BOOK COVERS

■ Fill in the boxes to give information about the books you look at.

| PRICE | | | | | |
|---|---|---|---|---|---|
| FICTION OR NON-FICTION | | | | | |
| PUBLISHER | | | | | |
| ILLUSTRATOR/ PHOTOGRAPHER | | | | | |
| AUTHOR'S NAME | | | | | |
| TITLE OF BOOK | | | | | |

# QUESTIONS

## OBJECTIVES

| UNIT | SPELLING AND VOCABULARY | GRAMMAR AND PUNCTUATION | COMPREHENSION AND COMPOSITION |
|---|---|---|---|
| WRITING NON-FICTION Questions. | Spell words beginning with the phoneme *wh*. Recognize and form questions using *what, why, where, which* and *who*. | Write in clear sentences using capital letters and full stops accurately. Turn statements into questions. Use question marks. | Reinforce and apply word level skills through shared and guided reading. Apply phonological, graphic knowledge and sight vocabulary to spell words accurately. |

## ORGANIZATION (3 HOURS)

| | INTRODUCTION | WHOLE-CLASS SKILLS WORK | DIFFERENTIATED GROUP ACTIVITIES | CONCLUSION |
|---|---|---|---|---|
| HOUR 1 | Shared look at words beginning with *wh*. | Shared writing of sentences. Discussion about spelling and punctuation. | 1: Write questions for each other and write answers. 2: Identify question sentences in text. 3*: Complete question sentences by adding words beginning with *wh*. | Reinforce spelling of words beginning with *wh*. Look at question sentences and question words. |
| HOUR 2 | Shared reading of 'Questions, questions, questions'. | Revision of spelling of questions. Create a class word bank. | 1: Complete question sentences by adding words beginning with *wh*. 2: Write questions for each other and write answers. 3*: Guided reading identifying question sentences in text. | Group 2 to read aloud answers for the rest of the class to identify questions. Shared writing of questions. |
| HOUR 3 | Shared look at a set of answers. Make up questions to go with each answer. | Shared writing with focus upon spelling and punctuation. | 1*: Guided reading identifying question sentences in text. 2: Complete question sentences by adding words beginning with *wh*. 3: Write questions for each other and write answers. | Look at and discuss Group 2's work on question sentences. Revision of punctuation for questions and spelling of question words. |

## RESOURCES

Photocopiable page 173 (Who, what, when, where, why?), photocopiable page 174 ('Questions, questions, questions'), a set of cards on which have been written the 'wh' question words, a set of answer sheets with 'wh' words, board or flip chart, Blu-Tack, paper, highlighter pens, writing materials.

## PREPARATION

Prepare enough copies of photocopiable page 173 (Who, what, when, where, why?) for each child to have one. Prepare an enlarged copy or OHT of photocopiable page 174 ('Questions, questions, questions') as well as enough copies for each child to have one. Prepare a set of answer sheets for Group 1 to use during Hour 1 by writing 'wh' words on alternate lines of ruled paper and the name of a child from another group at the top. Make a set of word cards with the 'wh' question words written on them. Have ready plenty of paper.

## Introduction and whole-class skills work

Ask the children a series of questions using 'what', 'why', 'where', 'which' and 'who'. Ask if anyone can tell you anything about the questions you are asking. Discuss with them the kinds of words which are often used to begin questions and show them some 'wh' words on cards.

Read the words with the children and then Blu-Tack each card to the board in turn and ask the children to make up some question sentences which begin with each word. As they do this, write some of the questions on the board immediately underneath the words, but do not, at this stage, add a question mark. If none of the children points out that a question mark is needed, ask them to think about what might be needed and show them a sample of text which has questions (you could use photocopiable page 174) and ask them to look carefully to see if something is missing from the sentences on the board.

Leave the cards with the 'wh' words on display so that all groups can see them easily.

## Differentiated group activities

1: Explain to the group that they will be writing questions for the other groups. Provide a sheet of paper for each child with the name of a member of another group written at the top. (If possible, provide a photograph of the child.) The paper should be lined and each alternate line should have a word beginning with 'wh' written on the left-hand side. Explain that the children should write a question sentence for each word and that they should leave a line between each sentence so that the child whose name is at the top may write answers in the spaces. Ask them to provide the answers on a separate sheet of paper.

2: Provide the children with copies of photocopiable page 174 ('Questions, questions, questions') and ask them to read through it carefully together and identify the question sentences. They should underline these and highlight the 'wh' word which begins each one. Encourage the children to look for other ways in which question sentences might begin (such as 'how'). If children complete the task early, they should go on to make up their own sentences beginning with 'wh' words and 'how'.

3*: Provide this group with copies of photocopiable page 173 (Who, what, when, where, why?) and ask them to fill in the missing 'wh' word for each question. Spend time talking through the sentences with them after reading or saying incomplete sentences to them orally.

## Conclusion

Ask Group 1 to read aloud some of the questions which they wrote and record some of these on the board. As you do so, ask children from Group 3 to help you with the spellings of the 'wh' words. Ask Group 2 to tell the class about the other words which they found which may begin question sentences. Finally, show everyone the text which Group 2 worked from and ask the whole class to read it and look for question sentences and question words.

## Introduction and whole-class skills work

Show the children an enlarged copy or OHT of photocopiable page 174 ('Questions, questions, questions') and read it to them. Re-read it with the children's help and ask three children to take the parts of mother, father and Lee and to read the words which they spoke, but not the rest of the text. Use this opportunity to revise the use of speech marks.

Ask the children to look for some of the question sentences and to identify the key question words that begin with 'wh'. Ask the children to tell you about other words that begin with 'wh' and revise their spellings. Look at some of the other ways in which questions are introduced and talk about some of the verbs that are used to show that someone is asking a question. In the text these are 'asked' and 'enquired'. Look, too, at some of the verbs which show how Lee responded. In the text these are 'muttered', 'replied', 'answered' and 'said'. Add these words to the class word bank (see 'How to make a word bank', page 10 of the Introduction).

## Differentiated group activities

1: Cloze exercise using photocopiable page 173 (Group 3, Hour 1).
2: Writing questions and answers exercise (as Group 1, Hour 1).

3*: Identify questions exercise (as Group 2, Hour 1), but with guided reading using photocopiable page 174 and the children's reading books.

### Conclusion
Ask Group 2 to read aloud some of the answers which they wrote to each other's questions and invite the rest of the class to suggest what the questions might have been.

**HOUR 3**

### Introduction and whole-class skills work
Write some statements on the board or flip chart that could be answers to questions. These could be as follows:

> *seven*
> *after tea*
> *not until I can ride it safely*
> *Tom*
> *75 centimetres*

Ask the children to try to think of questions to which these statements could be the answers and write these on the board or flip chart. Pay particular attention to discussion of the spellings of the key question words and the punctuation of questions.

Invite the children to think of other answers and write these on the board before asking the class to think of questions. You might allow the child who has suggested an answer to come out and ask others to provide questions before saying which question he or she had in mind.

### Differentiated group activities
1*: Guided reading and identifying questions exercise (as Group 3, Hour 1).
2: Cloze exercise (as Group 1, Hour 2).
3: Writing questions and answers exercise (as Group 2, Hour 2).

### Conclusion
Look at the question sentences which Group 1 identified and add any new question words to the word bank and discuss their spellings. Look again at the punctuation of questions and at the spellings of all the words in the word bank.

# WHO, WHAT, WHEN, WHERE, WHY?

■ Use the words in the box to complete each question sentence.

| who | what | when | where | why |
|-----|------|------|-------|-----|

_____ is your favourite food?

_____ do you live?

_____ do you like best: chips or boiled potatoes?

_____ is your birthday?

_____ is your best friend?

_____ do you like your best friend so much?

_____ are you going for a holiday?

_____ is the name of your teacher?

_____ does school start in the morning?

_____ time do you go to bed at night?

# QUESTIONS, QUESTIONS, QUESTIONS

Lee sat in an armchair with his face hidden in his hands.

"Whatever is the matter?" asked his mother.

"Nothing," muttered Lee.

"Why don't you go out to play?" asked his father.

"I don't want to," replied Lee quietly.

"Don't you feel very well?" enquired his mother.

"I'm all right," answered Lee.

"Have you fallen out with your friends, Lee?" asked Dad.

"I've only fallen out with one of them," replied Lee crossly.

"Which one?" said both his parents at once.

"Sarah," answered Lee.

"What happened? Why did you argue?" asked his mother.

"She said I hadn't scored a goal and I had. She said the ball went over the post but I know it went into the goal," said Lee angrily.

"What were you using for a goal post then?" asked Dad.

"We used our coats. We just put them on the ground a few metres apart," replied Lee.

"Do you know what we used to do when we were your age and there was an argument about whether the ball went in the goal or not?" asked Mum.

"No. What did you do, Mum?"

"We used to let the person who claimed to have scored take a penalty. If a goal was scored from the penalty the other shot counted as a goal. If the penalty was missed the goal didn't count," said Mum.

"That sounds like a good idea," said Lee.

"Why don't you go and tell Sarah about it? I bet you'll be friends again in five minutes if you do," said Dad.

Lee was suddenly much more cheerful. He said goodbye to his parents and dashed out to the park next door to find Sarah and the rest of his friends. "Sometimes parents can be quite clever!" he thought as he ran towards the footballers.

# A NIGHT OUT

## OBJECTIVES

| UNIT | SPELLING AND VOCABULARY | GRAMMAR AND PUNCTUATION | COMPREHENSION AND COMPOSITION |
|---|---|---|---|
| READING AND WRITING FICTION 'A Night Out'. | Secure knowledge of the spellings of the words in List 1 of the National Literacy Strategy. | Read aloud with intonation and expression. | Reinforce and apply word level skills through shared and guided reading. Apply phonological and graphic knowledge and sight vocabulary to spell words accurately. |

## ORGANIZATION (5 HOURS)

| | INTRODUCTION | WHOLE-CLASS SKILLS WORK | DIFFERENTIATED GROUP ACTIVITIES | CONCLUSION |
|---|---|---|---|---|
| HOUR 1 | Shared reading of 'A Night Out'. Discussion about possible endings. | Look at the spellings of words in the text which appear in the high frequency List 1. | 1: Use a selection of words to write an ending to the story. 2: Read text and identify words. 3*: Guided reading of 'A Night Out'. Focus upon intonation and expression. | Discuss the story endings written by Group 1. Look at the spelling of selected words from List 1. |
| HOUR 2 | Shared re-reading of 'A Night Out'. | Look again at the spellings of words in the text which appear in the high frequency List 1. | 1*(first): Guided reading of 'A Night Out'. Focus upon intonation and expression. 2*(second): Use a selection of words to write an ending to the story. 3: Read text and identify words. | Group 2 to read endings to story to the rest of the class. Look at initial phonemes and spellings. |
| HOUR 3 | Shared sentence-making activity. | Look at initial sounds, blends and digraphs. | 1: Make up sentences using words from List 1. 2*(first): Match words from List 1. 3*(second): Alphabetize words. | Read and alphabetize List 1 words from cards. |
| HOUR 4 | Look at high frequency words and at dictionary definitions. | Sort high frequency words according to various criteria. | 1: Sort words into groups and write sentences justifying groupings. 2*: Make a word bank using words from List 1. 3: Learn spellings in pairs. | Look at dictionary definitions of words produced by Group 2. |
| HOUR 5 | Look at another page from a dictionary. Discuss definitions and spellings. | Look at spellings of months of the year. | 1: Add to word banks of words from List 1. 2: Sort words into groups and write sentences justifying groupings. 3*: Make up sentences using words from List 1. | Look at dictionary definitions. Revise spellings of the months of the year. |

LIVERPOOL JOHN MOORES UNIVERSITY
LEARNING SERVICES

### RESOURCES

Photocopiable page 180 ('A Night Out'), photocopiable page 181 (Common words from 'A Night Out'), photocopiable page 182 (Words We Often Use), photocopiable page 183 ('The Months of the Year'), a set of coloured word cards, a simple children's dictionary, board or flip chart, OHP and acetate, Blu-Tack, the children's reading books, highlighter pens, writing materials

### PREPARATION

Prepare a set of photocopiable pages 180, 181 and 182 for each child in the class. Prepare enlarged copies or OHTs of all four photocopiable pages. Make a set of word cards from List 1 by writing the words on different coloured pieces of card, and then divide these into three sets. Enlarge at least two pages from the dictionary for class work. Display photocopiable page 182 for the whole class to refer to. Have ready the children's reading books and plenty of paper for the children to sort words and write definitions on.

### Introduction and whole-class skills work

Read the story 'A Night Out' from photocopiable page 180 to the children before showing an enlarged copy or OHT to them. Encourage them to discuss possible endings. Write notes showing some of the children's ideas and then re-read the story with them, helping them with unfamiliar words. These might include:

| | | | | | |
|---|---|---|---|---|---|
| o'clock | grandmother | whispered | annoying | wonderful | argue |
| threw | favourite | elephant | fingers | admit | crashing |

Discuss the spellings of some of the words which appear in the children's suggestions for the ending of the story and write these on the board or flip chart in order to provide a word bank for Groups 1 and 2 who will be writing endings to the story in the first two lessons.

Show the children an enlarged copy or OHT of photocopiable page 181 (Common words from 'A Night Out') – which is a list of words which appear both in the story and in List 1 – and discuss their spellings. Ask the children to suggest other sentences in which these words might be used. Write some of the sentences on the board or flip chart and discuss the spellings with the children as you do so.

### Differentiated group activities

1: Provide the children with copies of a selection of words to write an ending for the story. Discuss words which might be useful with the whole class before group work begins. Ask them to write at least six sentences and encourage them to check their spellings against the list which you have provided and against List 1 (photocopiable page 182). Some pairs of children from Group 1 could use the computer for this activity. Ask them to write their stories using word processing and encourage the use of a spell checker.

2: Provide the children with copies of photocopiable page 180 ('A Night Out') and ask them to read it and to find words listed on photocopiable page 181 (Common words from 'A Night Out'). When they have found the words, they should underline or highlight them. Ask them to use some of the words to write sentences.

3*: Provide the children with copies of the story 'A Night Out' and re-read it with them and use the opportunity to help them to read and spell high frequency words and any new and unfamiliar words.

### Conclusion

Discuss the story endings written by Group 1 and look at the spelling of selected words from List 1. Show the children how to use the *look, say, cover, write and check* method to learn to spell words and to help them to identify the most difficult parts of words so that they can focus upon those when learning to spell them.

### Introduction and whole-class skills work

Begin the lesson by re-reading 'A Night Out' with the children and by discussing content and any other endings which the children may suggest.

The focus for this lesson should be to involve the children in discussions about the high frequency words which appear in the text, and to give them opportunities to construct sentences using them. Talk with them about the structure of the words and ask them to identify those which are phonically regular and irregular. Talk with them about the words which obey the most common phonic rules and ask them to identify these. These include:

up    at    am    get    but    much    seen    time    with

Next, ask them to pick out the words which have less familiar graphemes representing phonemes. For example:

said    you    to    come    was    brother    don't
laugh    many    once    one    people    school    should    some
their    two    want    water    were    who    your

Once again, use the *look, say, cover, write and check* method to help the children to learn to spell the words and focus upon the difficult parts of the words. For example, in 'school' look at the 'k' phoneme and discuss the fact that it is represented by the grapheme 'ch'.

### Differentiated group activities
1*(first): Guided reading with intonation and expression (as Group 3, Hour 1).
2*(second): Write an ending to the story (as Group 1, Hour 1). Some pairs of children from Group 2 could use the computer for this activity.
3: Read text and identify words (as Group 2, Hour 1).

### Conclusion
Ask Group 2 to tell the rest of the class how they think the story should end. Look at some of the words which have presented problems to the children and work with the board or flip chart class to show the class how to spell them. Pay particular attention to initial phonemes and encourage children to sound these with you.

### Introduction and whole-class skills work

Tell the children that you have three sets of words each on different coloured card. Ask three children to come out holding their sets of words and let each in turn hold up words from their sets. Ask the class to say the words aloud. Discuss any words which present problems and use opportunities to look closely at graphemes and their phonemes.

Next, ask each of the three children to shuffle his or her words and then hold up the ones which are on the top of the piles. Invite other children to make up sentences which include all three words. Write the sentences on the board or flip chart and ask the children to help you to spell some of the words. Encourage them to use the names of the letters rather than their common sounds, but discuss the common sounds with the children and the sound which can be made when two letters combine to make a digraph or a blend.

### Differentiated group activities

1: Provide the children with copies of photocopiable page 181 (Common words from 'A Night Out') and ask them to make up sentences which include at least one of the words. You could add a competitive element by awarding a point for each of the words which they manage to include in a sentence and spell correctly.

2*(second): Show the children an enlarged copy or OHT of the full List 1, reproduced on photocopiable page 182 (Words We Often Use). Ask the children to look at their reading books and to identify words which appear there and on the list. Each time they find a word they could write it on the left-hand side of a page and then keep a tally of the number of times which it appears.

3*(first): Give the group the sets of word cards and let the children take turns to choose a card from each of the three piles. They should then place the words on the table in alphabetical order and write them out, taking care to spell them accurately. You may encourage them to use the *look, say, cover, write and check* method to do this.

### Conclusion

Use the three sets of cards again and ask the children to take turns to show a card to the class and read the word aloud. When all three children are holding up cards ask the class to help arrange the children in order according to the alphabetical order of the cards which they are showing. When the order has been ascertained, the children should change places so that the words read alphabetically from left to right.

### Introduction and whole-class skills work

Show the children an enlarged page of a simple dictionary and discuss its layout and the way in which definitions are written. Ensure that the page includes some words which appear in List 1 and look especially at the way in which these words are defined. A page from the H, M or T sections would be useful since words beginning with these letters are well-represented in List 1.

Discuss words from the sets of cards which were used in the previous lesson and use Blu-Tack to put some of them on display. Ask the children to look at the words and to suggest which have something in common. For example, they might look at the letters which words begin with, the medial sounds, terminal sounds, digraphs or meanings.

Discuss the fact that words could be grouped in many different ways and change groupings as children make new suggestions.

### Differentiated group activities

1: Provide the children with sets of high frequency words written on cards and ask them to work in pairs or small groups to sort the words into groups and to write sentences explaining their groupings. For example, they might group 'came', 'some', 'here', 'made' and 'make' together because they all end with an 'e'. They might group 'came', 'like', 'made' and 'time' together because they all have long vowel sounds.

2*: Show the children the enlarged copy of List 1 (photocopiable page 182) and ask them to work with you to create definitions for some of the words shown. Focus upon nouns and verbs as these may be easier to define. Each definition should be accompanied by a sentence which includes the word being defined. For example:

Dog    *A four-legged animal which is often kept as a pet.*
       *My pet dog has a loud bark and he wags his tail when he's happy.*

Some pairs of children from Group 2 could use the computer for this activity and could create entries which could contribute to a class dictionary.

3: Give pairs of children copies of photocopiable page 181 (Common words from 'A Night Out') and ask them to learn the spellings of the words listed. Encourage children to look closely at words and to use the *look, say, cover, write and check* method.

### Conclusion

Ask Group 2 to read out to the rest of the class the definitions and sentences that they have produced. Write the words on the board or flip chart and ask the class to help you to put these into alphabetical order.

### Introduction and whole-class skills work

Look again at the enlarged dictionary page and discuss layout once more. Work with the children to produce some more definitions and focus upon spellings. You may wish to look at a different page in this lesson.

Show the children an enlarged copy or OHT of photocopiable page 183 ('The Months of the Year'). Point out that the months all have capital letters. Use the rhyme of the months and discuss the order in which the words appear in the rhyme and how it differs from the order in the year.

Children could look at the words in groups and might learn to spell those which end with '-ember' separately from those which do not. March, May and June could be related to words in List 1 such as 'much', 'may' and (for June) words which end with an 'e' and have a long medial vowel sound. August may be related to other 'au' words which feature in the text 'Four Apples Fall' which appears in Term 2 (see pages 99 and 100).

### Differentiated group activities

1: Add to class dictionary (as Group 1, Hour 4)
2: Sorting words activity. Write sentences justifying groupings (as Group 1, Hour 4).
3*: Make up sentences using words from List 1(as Group 1, Hour 3).

### Conclusion

Look at the dictionary definitions produced by Group 1 and add these to the class dictionary. Revise the spellings of the months of the year using the rhyme on photocopiable page 183.

**Note:** Further literacy hours could be developed along similar lines using colours, days of the week and numbers (all of which feature in the 'plus' section of List 1.

# A NIGHT OUT

It was about twelve o'clock at night when Tom and Kate got home. Their sister, Jane, had been asleep since eight o'clock and the house was dark and quiet.

"Be very quiet," said their mum. "We don't want to wake Jane or your grandmother, do we?"

Dad closed the door as quietly as he could and then whispered, "You two are going to bed now. It's school in the morning and little boys and girls should be fast asleep by this time of night!"

Kate and Tom hated it when their father called them little boys and girls. They knew he was only trying to make them laugh and they loved him very much, but he could be very annoying at times.

"Come on, get up those stairs and clean your teeth, and don't run the water too loudly or you'll wake people up!" said Mum.

The brother and sister did as they were told. They were too tired to argue and besides it had been a wonderful evening. First they had been to a café and had eaten cake and drunk some tea. Next they had been to the circus. The clowns had made them laugh when they tipped water over one another and fell about on the ground and threw custard pies at each other. There had been many animals, but the children's favourite was the elephant who drank water and then blew it out of his trunk at the clowns. They had never seen Mum laugh so much.

After the circus, Mum drove them home, but on the way they stopped for fish and chips. Mum didn't want the car to smell of fish and chips, so they had walked up and down the street eating the hot food out of trays with their fingers. Dad had said that it was the only way to eat fish and chips and the children had to admit that food had never tasted so good.

Now they were back at their house and all they wanted to do was go to bed and think about the circus and fall asleep. Just as they were getting into bed they heard a loud crashing noise. Kate and Tom ran to the window at once and when they looked out they could not believe what they saw.

# COMMON WORDS FROM 'A NIGHT OUT'

**a**
a
about
after
all
and
are
as
at

**b**
back
be
bed
been
boy
brother
but
by

**c**
call(ed)
come
could

**d**
dad
did
do
don't
door
down

**f**
first
for

**g**
get
girl
go
going
good
got

**h**
had
he
him
his
home
house

**i**
in
it

**j**
just

**l**
laugh
little
look
love

**m**
made
make
many
much
mum

**n**
next
night
not
now

**o**
of
on
once
one
or
out
over

**p**
people

**r**
ran

**s**
said
saw
school
seen
should
sister
so
some

**t**
that
the
their
them
then
they
this
time
to
too
two

**u**
up

**v**
very

**w**
want
was
water
way
we
were
what
when
who
with

**y**
you
your

# WORDS WE OFTEN USE

| | | | | |
|---|---|---|---|---|
| a | day | in | old | these |
| about | did | is | on | they |
| after | dig | it | once | this |
| again | do | jump | one | three |
| all | dog | just | or | time |
| am | don't | last | our | to |
| an | door | laugh | out | too |
| and | down | like | over | took |
| another | first | little | people | tree |
| are | for | live(d) | play | two |
| as | from | look | push | up |
| at | get | love | pull | us |
| away | girl | made | put | very |
| back | go | make | ran | want |
| ball | going | man | said | was |
| be | good | many | saw | water |
| because | got | may | school | way |
| bed | had | me | see | we |
| been | half | more | seen | went |
| big | has | much | she | were |
| boy | have | mum | should | what |
| brother | help | must | sister | when |
| but | he | my | so | where |
| by | her | name | some | who |
| call(ed) | here | new | take | will |
| came | him | next | than | with |
| can | his | night | that | would |
| can't | home | no | the | yes |
| cat | house | not | their | you |
| come | how | now | them | your |
| could | I | of | then | |
| dad | if | off | there | |

# THE MONTHS OF THE YEAR

Thirty days have September,
April, June and November.
All the rest have thirty-one,
Except February alone.
Which has twenty-eight days clear,
And twenty-nine each leap year.

# COMMON SUFFIXES

## OBJECTIVES

| UNIT | SPELLING AND VOCABULARY | GRAMMAR AND PUNCTUATION | COMPREHENSION AND COMPOSITION |
|------|-------------------------|-------------------------|-------------------------------|
| READING AND WRITING NON-FICTION Word recognition and graphic knowledge. | Spell words with common suffixes. | Use standard forms of verbs in speaking and writing. | Reinforce and apply word level skills through shared and guided reading. |

## ORGANIZATION (2 HOURS)

| | INTRODUCTION | WHOLE-CLASS SKILLS WORK | DIFFERENTIATED GROUP ACTIVITIES | CONCLUSION |
|---|--------------|------------------------|--------------------------------|------------|
| HOUR 1 | Shared writing of sentences. | Look at spellings of words which add suffixes. | 1*: Guided reading. Identify suffixes. 2: Adding suffixes to words. 3: Match words with suffixes to their root words. | Look at examples of suffixes found by Group 1 and discuss spellings. |
| HOUR 2 | Shared exercise matching root words with suffixes. | Close look at the ways in which suffixes affect the spelling of words. | 1: Write sentences using a selection of word with suffixes. 2*: Guided reading. Identify suffixes. 3: Adding suffixes to words. | Look at sentences which Group 3 have produced and discuss their answers. Discuss the effects of changing words within a sentence. |

## RESOURCES

Photocopiable page 187 (Adding Suffixes), a list of common words which take the suffixes '-ed', '-ly' or '-ful', a set of cards on which have been written root words and root words with suffixes, several copies of the same reading book, writing materials.

## PREPARATION

Make enough copies of photocopiable page 187 for Groups 2 and 3 to use. Have ready several copies of the same reading book for Group 1 to use. Make a set of cards (enough for one for each child) on which have been written common words in their root form and the same words with one of the three suffixes '-ed', '-ly' or '-ful' added on. Have in mind a piece of text in the children's reading books which contains words with suffixes and words to which suffixes can be added.

### Introduction and whole-class skills work

This lesson is designed to encourage children to understand the purpose of suffixes, the ways in which they subtly change the meanings of words, and the rules for spelling words which add suffixes.

Show the children a list on the board or flip chart of words such as:

| | | | |
|---|---|---|---|
| *help* | *use* | *hope* | *hate* |
| *mouth* | *wonder* | *bad* | *mad* |
| *sad* | *usual* | *clever* | *smooth* |

Discuss the words and their meanings and ask the children to help you to write sentences which include each of them. For example, you might write: *I help my dad with the washing up.* You could then ask the children how you should write the sentence if you wanted to show that you had already helped your dad. The sentence might then become: *I helped my dad with the washing up.* This could lead to your asking the children if they could think of a word with 'help' in it which described someone who helped a lot. This should lead the children towards the word 'helpful'. They could then help you to write a sentence which includes the word 'helpful'. Discuss the spelling of 'helpful' and make it clear that words which add '-ful' end with only one 'l'.

Tell them that the meanings of the words can be changed slightly by adding suffixes such as '-ed', '-ful' and '-ly'. Write some sentences on the board or flip chart and add suffixes to some of the words. Discuss the fact that in places the sentences no longer make sense when this is done. Ask the children to suggest how the sentences could be changed so that they do make sense.

### Differentiated group activities

1*: Give the group several copies of the same reading book and ask the children to scan a piece of text for words with suffixes. Ask them to write down the words they find. Read through the text with the group before asking them to take turns to read.

2: Provide the group with copies of photocopiable page 187 (Adding Suffixes). Encourage the children to discuss the possible suffixes which might be added to the words in bold type before deciding which one to choose in each case. Some pairs of children from Group 2 could use the computer for this activity if you make a file with the sentences from the worksheet.

3: This group will be doing an activity which the whole class will be attempting during the following lesson. By trying it before the other children, Group 3 may be better able to undertake the class work and may also be able to show the others how to do the activity. Provide the group with some cards with root words and words with suffixes and ask them to match the words, such as matching 'help' to 'ed' to make 'helped'. This will involve sorting, discussion and, if you think it appropriate, recording.

### Conclusion

Write on the board or flip chart some of the words which Group 1 discovered during their group reading session. Discuss spellings and highlight the changes which are made to some words when '-ed' is added.

### Introduction and whole-class skills work

Provide each child with two cards: one with a root word and the other with a root word with a suffix added. The words may be given out randomly and it does not matter if a child has a word with a suffix and also the same root word.

Ask the children to look carefully at their words and invite some to read them aloud. Ask one child to come to the front and hold up his root word. Now ask who has a word which derives from the word and has a suffix. When the word has been found, ask the children to stand next to each other at the front and show their cards. Discuss the change to the root word and look at the spellings with the class. Continue the activity and find several more examples.

When the children have become familiar with their words, ask questions such as:

*Who has the word which begins with 'w' and means 'extremely good'?*
*Who has a word which begins with 'l' and means 'used to like'?*

Ask children to hold up their word cards if they think they have the word you are looking for. Some classes may be able to develop the activity so that the children make up questions about their own words and the others have to work out which word they have. For example:

*My word begins with 'u' and means 'most often'. What is it?*

### Differentiated group activities

1: Ask the children to choose words from the selection of cards and to try to use as many as possible in sentences, which they should write down.
2*: Group reading exercise (as Group 1, Hour 1).
3: Exercise using photocopiable page 187 (as Group 2, Hour 2).

### Conclusion

Ask Group 3 to read aloud the sentences which they have worked on. Discuss the words they have used and their appropriateness. Talk about spellings again and emphasize once more the single 'l' in the suffix '-ful' and the way in which some verbs change when '-ed' is added.

# ADDING SUFFIXES

■ Fill in the blanks by adding **-ed**, **-ly** or **-ful**.

Simon is a very **help** person.
Simon is a very **help**_____ person.

Nicola **help** her teacher to give out pencils yesterday.
Nicola **help**_____ her teacher to give out pencils yesterday.

Mary behaved very **bad** last week.
Mary behaved very **bad**_____ last week.

Mark is **usual** a very kind boy.
Mark is **usual**_____ a very kind boy.

Jenny **use** to live in London.
Jenny **use**_____ to live in London.

Raj had a **mouth** of chips.
Raj had a **mouth**_____ of chips.

Danny **jump** in the air when his team scored a goal.
Danny **jump**_____ in the air when his team scored a goal.

Alex walked **sad** to his car after his football team lost.
Alex walked **sad**_____ to his car after his football team lost.

The big chocolate cake was a **wonder** sight.
The big chocolate cake was a **wonder**_____ sight.

Each slice of cake **taste** even more **love** than the last one.
Each slice of cake **taste** even more **love**_____ than the last one.

# PAST AND PRESENT

## OBJECTIVES

| UNIT | SPELLING AND VOCABULARY | GRAMMAR AND PUNCTUATION | COMPREHENSION AND COMPOSITION |
|------|------------------------|------------------------|-------------------------------|
| READING FICTION AND POETRY 'Clare and Tim'. | Secure reading and spelling of high frequency words. | Use the past tense consistently for narration. | Notice the difference between spoken and written forms. |

## ORGANIZATION (3 HOURS)

| | INTRODUCTION | WHOLE-CLASS SKILLS WORK | DIFFERENTIATED GROUP ACTIVITIES | CONCLUSION |
|---|---|---|---|---|
| **HOUR 1** | Shared reading of 'Clare and Tim'. Discussion about the text. | Discuss past and present tenses. | 1: Change text into past tense. 2: Read and retell story in own words. 3*: Group reading and discussion about past and present tenses. | Group 2 to retell the story in their own words to the rest of the class and write down some of the verbs they use. The rest of the class to identify past and present tenses. |
| **HOUR 2** | Shared writing in the past tense. | Discuss spelling of verbs in the past and present tenses. | 1*: Write sentences in past and present tenses. 2: Change text into past tense. 3: Match verbs in past and present tense. | Group 1 to read aloud their writing to the rest of the class, who should identify the past or present tenses. |
| **HOUR 3** | Look at text from an early reader and change present tense to past tense. | Look at verbs in the high frequency List 1. Discuss spelling and changes of tense. | 1: Find examples of past and present tenses in books. 2*: Write sentences in past and present tenses. 3: Change text into past tense. | Look at Group 3's work on matching verbs. Look at the use of the |

## RESOURCES

Photocopiable page 191 ('Clare and Tim'), photocopiable page 192 containing verbs from the high frequency List 1 (Verbs We Often Use), photocopiable page 193 showing verbs in the past and present tenses (Past and Present), a piece of text from an early reader using the present tense (such as the *Fuzzbuzz* series), a grid such as that shown below (Hour 3), the children's reading books, board or flip chart, highlighter pens, writing materials.

## PREPARATION

Prepare sufficient copies of photocopiable page 191 for each child to have one as well as an enlarged version or OHT. Prepare copies of photocopiable page 193 (Past and Present) for Group 3 to use. Make an enlarged copy of a piece of text from an early reader. Draw a grid such as the one shown below and prepare copies Group 1 and draw an enlarged version on the board or flip chart. Have the children's reading books ready for them to consult as well as plenty of paper.

**Note:** The list shown on photocopiable page 192 is not an exhaustive list and it should be remembered that some verbs may be used as other parts of speech depending upon context. For example, 'name' could be a noun in 'His name is David' and a verb in 'I name this child David'.

## Introduction and whole-class skills work

**Note:** The lessons in this unit are designed to draw attention to the use of the past tense in narrative. It is unusual to find the present tense used in stories except within speech marks. However, some early reading scheme books are written in the present tense and it is possible that some children may still be using these. The books may be a useful resource for this lesson. When changing text into the past tense, children should be aware that speech should remain unaltered.

Begin by reading the story 'Clare and Tim' (photocopiable page 191) and ask the children what they notice about it. Next, ask them to retell you the story. As they do so, write some of the things they say on the board or flip chart. It is very likely that they will relate the story in the past tense and examples of this should be recorded on the board for later discussion.

Show the children an enlarged version or OHT of the story and ask them if they have any comments on the way in which it is written. Draw their attention to the sentences which you wrote down and compare them with those in the story. Ask the children if they can tell the difference and introduce the idea of writing as if something has happened already and as if it is happening now.

Look at the first part of the story and ask children to volunteer to re-read it and change the verbs into the past tense. Whenever a verb is changed, make a note of it in both its past and present tense forms. For example, 'go/went', 'ride/rode', 'are/were'.

Ask the children to make up sentences orally which include each form, and phrase your questions so that the ideas of past and present tense are constantly reinforced. For example: *Who can say a sentence with 'went' in it to show that something has already happened?*

## Differentiated group activities

1: Give the children copies of photocopiable page 191 ('Clare and Tim') and ask them to find and underline or highlight the verbs and then write the past tense versions above each one. Pairs of children could use the computer for this activity if the text is saved as a file which they can then manipulate to change tenses.

2: Give the children copies of photocopiable page 191 and ask them to read and retell the story in their own words. Ask the children to write the story in about eight sentences and encourage them to tell the story in the past tense.

3*: Ask the children to look through their reading books and to read (or re-read) simple stories as a group. Encourage them to discuss past and present tenses. When you have worked with the children for ten minutes you may wish to work with Group 2 to help them to write sentences in the past tense. Group 3 should then spend time looking in their reading books for some common verbs in the past tense form. These could include the following:

| | | | |
|---|---|---|---|
| *looked* | *liked* | *went* | *was* |
| *saw* | *did* | *had* | *made* |
| *took* | *were* | *called* | |

## Conclusion

Ask Group 2 to retell the story in their own words and write some of the verbs which they used on the board. Show the class an enlarged version of a simple piece of text and ask Groups 1 and 3 to identify past and present tenses in the text or in sentences which you say aloud.

## Introduction and whole-class skills work

Begin by writing a sentence from the story 'Clare and Tim' on the board or flip chart and by asking the children to change it into the past tense. Repeat this using sentences which you have made up and which are relevant to the children. For example:

It is Sarah's birthday today.
John is wearing a red jumper.

When the children seem confident about using the past tense to change the sentences, ask them to help you to write a short story on the board. This may be an alternative version to, or extension of, 'Clare and Tim' or it could be a new story. As you write with the children, discuss tenses and the ways in which the verbs are spelled. In particular, look at the suffix '-ed' and ensure that children know how to use it accurately. Many of the most frequently used verbs are irregular and it would be a good idea to provide a word bank of these in their past and present tenses (see 'How to make a word bank, page 10 of the Introduction). Show them photocopiable page 192 (Verbs We Often Use) for some suggestions of common verbs from List 1, some of them with an irregular past tense, which could be used.

### Differentiated group activities

1*: Ask this group to make up sentences and to write these in the present tense and then in the past tense. Encourage the children to work in pairs and to discuss the words they use.

2: Changing text into the past tense (as Group 1, Hour 1).

3: Provide the children with copies of photocopiable page 193 (Past and Present) and ask them to match the pairs of verbs in past and present tense form.

### Conclusion

Ask Group 1 to read some of their sentences to the rest of the class without saying whether they are in the past or present tense and ask the children to identify the tenses. Draw attention to the matching of words in past and present tense forms which Group 3 have produced and make a list for display.

### Introduction and whole-class skills work

Find an example of an early reader which is written in the present tense. The *Fuzzbuzz* series (Oxford University Press, 1978) may be useful. Read one of the stories to the children and then ask them if they noticed anything about the way in which it was written. Show them an enlarged version of a page of the story and ask them to help you to change it into the past tense.

Look at the list of verbs which was begun in the previous lesson and ask the children to help you to add to it. Discuss spellings and talk about the words which change to the past tense by adding '-ed' and those which are irregular.

### Differentiated group activities

1: Ask this group to look at their own reading books and to find examples of common verbs in past and present tense form (such as those shown on photocopiable page 193). Draw out a grid as shown below, make enough copies for each child and ask the children to complete it.

|  | **FOUND IN SPEECH** | **NOT IN SPEECH** |
| --- | --- | --- |
| PRESENT TENSE VERBS |  |  |
| PAST TENSE VERBS |  |  |

2*: Changing text into the past tense (as Group 1, Hour 1).

3: Present this group with a list of sentences written on the board or flip chart which include the most common verbs and ask the children to rewrite the sentences using the past tense. Some pairs of children from Group 3 could use the computer for this activity.

### Conclusion

Draw a grid on the board or flip chart like the one used by Group 1 and ask the children to help you to fill it in. Ask Group 1 children to read aloud some of the sentences they found which include the verbs and discuss the way in which we tend to use the past tense in narration, but often the present tense in speech.

# CLARE AND TIM

Clare and Tim are good friends. They go everywhere together. They both have bikes.

Clare and Tim go on a bike ride with Tim's mother. They ride on a special path which is just for bikes. Cars are not allowed on the special cycle path.

Just as they are getting to Brimton where they are going to have a picnic, Clare hears a car horn. There is a car right behind them. The car is driven by an old man. He has glasses and he is going very slowly. He looks very cross.

When he gets near to Clare and Tim and Tim's mum they stop and get off their bikes.

The old man stops his car. He gets out and starts shouting.

"You are taking up all the road!" he shouts. "I can't get past you!"

"This isn't a road for cars," says Tim's mum. "This is a cycle path!"

The old man looks around him. He sees a blue and white sign. He goes right up to it to read it.

"Oh dear," he says. "I must have the wrong glasses on. I am very sorry."

Tim's mum shows the man how to get to the road. He drives very slowly and then he parks his car and walks back home to get his other glasses.

# VERBS WE OFTEN USE

| look | been | love |
| like | call | made |
| said | came | make |
| go | could | push |
| are | did | pull |
| going | do | put |
| play | dig | ran |
| am | got | saw |
| come | had | seen |
| get | has | should |
| went | have | take |
| was | help | took |
| see | jump | want |
| can | laugh | were |
| be | live | will |

# PAST AND PRESENT

■ Match the words in the present tense to those in the past tense. The first one has been done for you.

■ Note: Some past tense words have more than one present tense.

| PRESENT | PAST |
|---------|------|
| look ——————————— | looked |
| like | said |
| go | went |
| say | got |
| play | called |
| am | played |
| come | was |
| get | loved |
| see | saw |
| can | lived |
| call | ran |
| do | made |
| dig | were |
| has | came |
| have | could |
| help | did |
| jump | dug |
| laugh | helped |
| live | wanted |
| love | took |
| make | laughed |
| push | jumped |
| pull | pushed |
| take | pulled |
| want | liked |
| is | had |
| run | |

# TAKE A LETTER

## OBJECTIVES

| UNIT | SPELLING AND VOCABULARY | GRAMMAR AND PUNCTUATION | COMPREHENSION AND COMPOSITION |
|------|-------------------------|-------------------------|-------------------------------|
| READING FICTION AND POETRY Textual examination. | Reinforce work on discriminating syllables in reading and spelling. Secure phonemic spellings from the previous five terms. | Understand the use of capital letters and full stops. | Develop phonological, contextual and grammatical knowledge by demonstrating that letters can have different sounds according to context. |

## ORGANIZATION (2 HOURS)

| | INTRODUCTION | WHOLE-CLASS SKILLS WORK | DIFFERENTIATED GROUP ACTIVITIES | CONCLUSION |
|--|--------------|------------------------|--------------------------------|------------|
| HOUR 1 | Shared examination of a text with single letters and digraphs, moving on to words, phrases and sentences. | Talk about the function of phonemes and graphemes and the effects of context. | 1: Look at compound sentences and distinguish their component parts. 2*: Guided look at compound sentences and distinguish their component parts. 3: Find words and graphemes within words. | Select pupils from each of the group to read and present their work to the rest of the class. Discuss responses. Display some compound sentences. |
| HOUR 2 | Shared examination of a text which has all but a few graphemes and words covered up. | Look at the phonemes in List 3 and match them to words. | 1: Find words containing graphemes from List 3 in reading books. 2: Find words and graphemes within words. 3*: Guided look at compound sentences and distinguish their component parts. | Shared look at List 1 and other words from the word bank. Identify words containing specific graphemes and phonemes. |

## RESOURCES
A set of sentences which include the phonemes with which Year 2 should by now be familiar (List 3 of the National Literacy Strategy), a means of covering parts of the sentences so as to reveal them gradually (such as an appropriately-sized piece of card), a copy of a page of text (you could use an appropriate photocopiable page from any of the previous units), a word bank based upon List 1, Group 1's reading books, Blu-Tack, highlighter pens, writing materials.

## PREPARATION

Prepare a set of sentences which include words containing phonemes from List 3 and make sufficient copies for each child to have one. Make an enlarged copy of a piece of text (such as an appropriate photocopiable page from a previous unit) with all but a few graphemes and words covered with pieces of card stuck on with Blu-Tack. Prepare a word bank based upon List 1 (see 'How to make a word bank', page 10 of the Introduction). Either photocopy a piece of text from Group 1's reading books for them to use during Hour 2 or have the books ready for them to consult directly.

### Introduction and whole-class skills work
This activity is designed to develop phonological, contextual and grammatical knowledge by demonstrating that letters can have different sounds according to context and that the meanings attached to words and phrases can be determined by the surrounding text.

If you have an OHP, make a series of OHTs which show, respectively a single letter, a digraph, a word, a compound word which includes the word, a phrase or clause, a sentence and a paragraph. If you do not have an OHP, you could achieve a similar effect by producing an enlarged version of the paragraph and covering parts of it with card. An example could be as follows:

- e
- he
- head
- headteacher
- the headteacher is mad
- the headteacher is made in Japan
- the present I gave to the headteacher is made in Japan
- Tom thinks the present I gave to the headteacher is made in Japan, but I made it myself.

Talk with the children about being reading 'detectives' and explain that there are clues all around when they meet a word which they cannot read or do not understand in a book. In looking at the sentences and parts of sentences, encourage them to look for capital letters and punctuation to give clues as to the positioning of words and their usage. For example, in the text above 'the' before 'present' does not have a capital letter so it cannot begin a sentence and there is no full stop after 'Japan' so we know that that is not the end of a sentence.

### Differentiated group activities
1: Provide this group with copies of some compound sentences and ask the children to look for a letter, then a digraph, then part of a word and so on. (A compound sentence contains two or more main clauses, such as *John was a good boy and he always helped his father with the cooking*.) Ask them to write each part down in turn and then to invite friends to guess at what the whole sentence might be from looking at the successive parts.
2*: This group's work will be similar to that done by Group 1 except that it will be guided by the teacher.
3: Provide this group with a word bank based upon List 1 and including other words which the children have recently met, and ask them to find graphemes within words. They should write the words down and underline the graphemes.

### Conclusion

Ask each group to tell the rest of the class about the work which has been done and provide another example for the children to discuss. Display some of the compound sentences.

### Introduction and whole-class skills work

Begin the lesson as you did the last one by introducing a single letter or grapheme from a sentence and asking the children to make guesses as to which word, phrase and sentence it might be part of as you gradually reveal more clues.

Now show the children an enlarged piece of text which has all but a few graphemes and words covered with pieces of card stuck on with Blu-Tack. The words which are uncovered should provide clues as to the content of the text and the graphemes should be chosen from the following:

| oo | u | ar | oy | oi | ow | air | or | are | ear |
|----|----|----|----|----|----|----|----|----|----|
| ere | oor | aw | au | ore | er | ir | ur | ea | |

Have a copy of the word bank on display so that the children can match the graphemes to words and ask them to suggest what the words might be. Gradually reveal more and more of the text and encourage the children to predict what it might be about and the exact wording. Talk with the children about the words and their spellings and about the different ways in which phonemes may be represented by graphemes.

### Differentiated group activities

1: Ask the children to use their reading books or other appropriate text to find words from List 1. If the text is photocopied, they could highlight the words or they could list them underneath the graphemes.

2: Finding graphemes within words from a word bank (as Group 3, Hour 1).

3*: Exercise using compound sentences (as Group 1, Hour 1).

### Conclusion

Look at List 1 and other words from the class word bank and identify words which contain specified graphemes and phonemes. Look, in particular, at words which include the same grapheme but are pronounced differently.